MIRTH AND MUSINGS

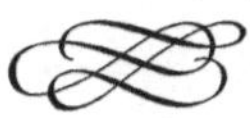

SANDI HOOVER

JIM TRITTEN

Mirth and Musings

Published by Red Penguin Books

Bellerose Village, New York

Library of Congress Control Number: 2021913522

ISBN

Print 978-1-63777-108-2

Digital 978-1-63777-109-9

CONTENTS

"DAD, I'M ON AN ALL-PLANT DIET"

JIM TRITTEN

"Dad, I'm on an all-plant diet." These were the words my son greeted me with when we met in Silver City, New Mexico, in September. It was not exactly the kind of greeting I'd expected when we planned a family weekend together for our wives and ourselves. We'd driven about halfway between where we live in Corrales, New Mexico, and where they lived in Tucson, Arizona. We were to spend three nights together at the Gila River Festival. I'd envisaged talking, walking outdoors, relaxing, and some eating and drinking. But eating real *man's* food, not some wishy-washy vegan fare served by unshaven armpit and stubbly-legged tree-hugging waitresses extolling the virtues and benefits of stuffing my face with chlorophyll, mosses, and algae.

OK, maybe I'm getting somewhat carried away after the fact. At the time, I confess I gave a more measured response to my son, "Good, I'll go all-plant too."

Good grief, *why* did I say that? What possibly prompted me to agree to abandon decades of moist meaty self-indulgence for what could not be any sane or rational reason? Was I really going to give up choice morsels of succulent slow-cooked pork shoulder to attempt to eat vegetables on their own, without even butter? I mean, really, have you ever tried Brussels sprouts by themselves? Try them instead, seared in a sizzling iron pan first coated with butter while being steamed in a thin layer of genuine chicken stock, and then garnished with a half-pound of bacon, shallots, and garlic. OK, I will admit shallots and garlic are plants, but they are serving their proper place in support of the bacon and butter and not in lieu of them.

Fortunately, when my son arrived, I'd already eaten my lunch of a turkey melt with Swiss cheese and green chili, so I did not have to deal with the plant diet thing until dinner. But here is the funny part. Before we arrived in Silver City, my son's wife asked me to order her a vegan meal at the Bear Mountain Lodge, where we stayed. The innkeeper had promised a wonderful vegan experience if she was given advance notice. We had actually all agreed in advance of our arrival to a vegan meal at dinner one evening.

A dinner…one meal…*not* the entire weekend!

Where did my son get this idea, and where the hell else was I going to find plant-based food in Silver City, New Mexico? Was I to go to the tofu-loving organic food co-op on North Bullard Street to traipse through the cornucopia of colorful plants and fruits that only excites the professional nutritionist?

A point of clarification for the other carnivores in the room. There are categories of plant-like foods available in many enlightened restaurants.

"Vegetarian" encompasses the practice of following plant-based diets that excludes all red meat, poultry, and seafood but, for many, includes dairy products (such as butter) and eggs. I suspect most people are familiar with the term vegetarian and may have even shared company with other humans who embrace the concept. They may have seen vegetarian options on restaurant menus. The subset of vegetarianism that includes dairy and eggs is termed *lacto-ovo-vegetarian* and is likely the type of vegetarian alternatives offered by most restaurants.

Vegan diets, on the other hand, eliminate all animal food products of any form. So, a vegan meal could not include dairy products or eggs, or any animal by-products such as honey. Although chocolate comes from the pod of the cocoa tree, most normal commercial chocolates have dairy and other processed ingredients as additives. Fortunately, vegan chocoholics enjoy a secure source of their addiction; there is an abundance of vegan chocolate available even in typical grocery stores and obviously, in health food stores. The vegan diet is considerably more difficult than the vegetarian. Some alternative restaurants will prepare vegan meals with twenty-four hours' notice.

Perhaps you have heard of the raw diet. Interestingly, although embraced by the same type of people who embrace vegetarian or vegan, the emphasis in raw diets is uncooked, unprocessed, and organic products for food. But the raw diet actually allows raw red meat (*carpaccio*), raw seafood (*sashimi*), raw dairy products (milk, cheese, yogurts), and raw eggs.

Now my son said he was on an all-plant diet, and this category is somewhat different from any of the above. Essentially, per his definition, if it did not come from a plant, it is not on the dinner table. So all-plant cannot include processed plants or cooking with the aid of dairy products such as butter. No *piñon* caramel ice cream. This diet is even more challenging than vegan and is almost impossible to do at restaurants. So, we compromised and moderated our goal to be an all-vegan weekend. Note I said *goal*.

Dinner was a success. I ate green things, orange things, brown things, red things, yellow things, white things, blue things, and I have to admit, they all had good flavors, smells, and tastes. However, the innkeeper had been cooking brisket all afternoon, and the aroma of the delicious meat wafting through the air during our vegan meal may have stimulated my appetite for plants or even improved their flavor. He brought me a sample of the wet brisket after the vegan dessert course, and naturally, I did not want to offend him, so I silently ate the offering and made suitable comments to him in the kitchen on how good it tasted. Despite this technical violation, we all declared success for the vegan meal and toasted our success with a glass of dry red wine. Hmmmmm, is red wine part of an all-plant diet?

Breakfast at the Lodge was a challenge. I watched in horror as my son basically ate bone-dry granola for his post-slumber banquet. I have to confess at this point, I embraced *lacto-ovo-vegetarian* as I feasted on scrambled eggs cooked in butter, butter on my toast, and cream in my coffee. The innkeeper hid a few scraps of turkey sausage under the eggs so that no one would see them—only a slight compromise. All-vegan had only been a goal, not an explicit objective.

I had a salad for lunch and noticed Diane's Restaurant had not sneaked in any chopped boiled eggs or shreds of cheese. I chewed, and chewed, and chewed. It was good…just healthy.

With advance notice, we had selected a restaurant in town for dinner that boasted of its vegan delights—the Curious Kumquat. The interesting part is we did not get the opportunity to order anything specifically—the order was for a vegan meal, and we would get whatever the chef thought would tickle his fancy. Interesting concept. Chef Rob Connoley introduced himself. An "All-American" looking young man, I would guess in his thirties, baseball cap always on, no facial hair. No fancy chef trousers. Can you trust a chef who wears a ball cap in the restaurant and doesn't sport the fancy chef trousers?

Again, I ate green things, orange things, brown things, red things, yellow things, white things, and blue things. The chef came out with each of five courses, made a magnificent speech about what we were about to consume, and presented something on a plate that looked truly spectacular and tasted great. Really, I mean it. The meal was terrific. And apparently vegan. I just ate and still have no idea what I ate. But it was a wonderful experience, and again we toasted our success with a glass of dry red wine—actually, two bottles. I'm sure wine is plant food. I guess you can't tell a chef by his hat.

There is precedent for including alcoholic beverages in restricted diets. German Paulaner monks fast durin

Lent by sustaining life with a specially brewed *doppelbock* beer with sufficient nutrients to support life during extended periods of soul-cleansing. From personal experience, I can attest it tastes quite different from any light lager beer familiar to the American palate. More like an alcoholic thick soup. Yup, I'm sure beer and wine are plant foods.

The following morning, breakfast was again a challenge. My wife and I slipped away under cover of dawn and roosters crowing [my son never gets up with the sun] to Nancy's Silver Café, where I enjoyed steak and runny eggs over-easy with beautifully golden hash browns, needing no enhancements like ketchup. Breakfast tasted great, and I took a picture then posted it on Facebook, just in case this was my last normal meal.

Salad at Vick's Eatery for lunch. With advance notice at Shevek & Co., we had another vegan dinner picked by a gourmet and rather eccentric chef. We got a full explanation from a man who looked like a chef. Had the chef's clothes, an accent, and wonderful stories about his ethnic derivation and influences on his preparations. No facial hair this time, but I later saw Chef Shevek Barnhart's photos with various hair lengths, beards, and mustaches. More speeches about the wonders of what we were about to partake in and incredible presentations actually making you want to indulge. Again, the flavors, smells, and tastes were superb. Could it be these vegan meals were worth writing home about? Do vegan chefs change their facial appearances as often as their menus?

The success of these vegan meals was beginning to make me doubt the value of our species having clawed its way to the top of the food chain. Was it time to consider grazing on a steady diet of plants? Was it time to give up *carne adovada* inside soft flour tortillas with over-easy eggs on top? Might I have had my last *pollo asada* slow-cooked overnight in chicken broth and then spread over Israeli couscous?

Our final meal together at the Lodge was breakfast. I again reverted to *lacto-ovo-vegetarian.* I'm sure the spuds were cooked with butter—they were delicious. The toast came with butter, and the eggs had cheese. Organic, of course. My son ate a raw fruit cup for breakfast. How was he going to sustain life?

He and his wife departed for Tucson, and my wife and I went touring to the Gila Cliff Dwellings. After sufficient time and distance, we were able to divorce ourselves from the vegan weekend. We returned to the Lodge and told the innkeeper I would gladly partake of the brisket we had smelled and sampled earlier. A full meal, not just a pity serving.

My main observations after a weekend of semi-vegan eating; if you go vegan or plant-based and plan to eat out, it is necessary to work with the establishment and give them twenty-four hours-notice or more. Having done this, you will likely find the chefs try harder and give you individual attention. The result is more enjoyable than just ordering meat and potatoes from the menu. The experience becomes more of a happening than a meal. And that's worth it in more ways than just what we put into our mouths.

I came to appreciate a new part of New Mexico. And, we had an enjoyable family weekend, which was the point. I experimented with some different foods and enjoyed every offering. Trying to eat out and maintain an all-plant diet is exceedingly tricky. I also confirmed what I already knew—I'm *never* going to live an all-plant lifestyle.

My son later abandoned his. I've never asked why.

Previously published in *More Voices of New Mexico*, Ruth E. Francis, Paul Rhetts and Barbe Awalt, eds., Los Ranchos, NM: Rio Grande Books, January 15, 2015, pp.173-177; in *Currents: Corrales Writing*

Group 2015 Anthology, Patricia Walkow, ed., North Charleston, SC: CreateSpace, October 4, 2015, pp. 11-16, and in *The Basil O' Flaherty*, November 11, 2016. A shorter version of this piece won 2nd Place and a Silver Medal at the National Veterans Creative Arts Competition in 2014. The full text was awarded an Honorable Mention in the New Mexico Press Women 2016 Communications Contest—Essay, chapter or section in a book.

GIVE IT AN INCH

SANDI HOOVER

One spring afternoon, William Mallon found a worn leather pouch tucked between field rocks in his garden wall. The stiff material resisted his tugs, but he finally got it open and poured the contents into his hand. His head swiveled suspiciously as if the person who had left them might suddenly appear and accuse him of stealing. *Just a bunch of tiny seeds. Will they grow? Wonder what they'll be.* He relaxed when, as usual, he did not see a soul in any direction. He thought perhaps a friend had left them as a joke.

But there was no one there to surprise him.

A loner, Mallon was confirmed in his bachelor status and liked his remote location. He had a large garden plot, merely feet from his kitchen door. That planting area had been hard-wrested from the rock-filled soil, now outlined by walls created from those same rocks. He took great pride in the quality and quantity of vegetables he harvested each year. Sturdy greenery was flourishing in neat rows, promising another fulfilling year.

Past his garden, his solitary house faced a slope dropping to a walled-off goat pen. Beyond was more pasture with black-faced sheep lying contented in deep clover, then a cliff edge with sea beyond. Below the cliff, out of sight, was his small boat, waiting for his frequent quick fishing jaunts to provide himself dinner.

But he had enough empty space at the back of his garden to plant another vegetable. He tossed the small seeds as he walked through the open area and stomped some dirt over them. *Old seeds, like their rotten bag. If they come up, fine, if not, fine, since I'm through planting this season.*

Almost daily, when not out fishing, he walked through his garden with a hoe in hand and removed any weed having the effrontery to ruin the pristine nature of his plot. The exception was off in the corner. Green sprouts had appeared, but he didn't bother weeding the unknown seed's space. He wasn't sure what the new plants would look like, and he hadn't been careful to put the seeds in rows. Whatever the green thing turned out to be, William could always feed the vegetable to his goats if it grew. *I'm sure my goats will eat it, weeds or not.*

As days passed, the green sprouts grew larger. *Those crinkled leaves are fancy, but I still don't recognize them. I'll leave 'em 'till they look big enough to eat. I'll take a few to my friend George, who knows all about plants.* He cut a couple to carry with him when he next went to town.

George gave his considered opinion: the plant was some sort of kale, but a variety he had never seen before. "Kale's reputed to be highly beneficial and healthy, but not high on the preferred list of vegetables."

Several days later, Mallon was looking across his garden, to the far edge. Plants he recognized in the strange patch were waving to and fro when nothing else showed movement. Shriveling and shrinking as he watched, they were dying. He saw the kale, as George called it, had grown around their base. *Are those leaves choking them? Are they eating the weeds? Whatever they're doing, it's helping me, so good for them.*

As days passed, Mallon's appreciation turned to concern as the plants spread. He took his hoe and went one evening on his normal rounds after missing days due to shearing sheep. He was startled to discover the unknown plant had crept into his veggie garden and was strangling a cabbage.

"I can't have this. You have to go!" William exclaimed as he hacked with his hoe at the offending leaves. They were tough to cut, but with repeated swings, he succeeded in separating the aggressive leaves from the rest of the deeply ruffled, blue-green bush.

Is it my imagination, or is it changing color? I'm sure it has gotten darker since I first hit it. He pulled the chopped-off leaves into a heap at the foot of the wall. Satisfied he had stopped the plant by pruning its encroaching leaves, Mallon puttered around the rest of the garden for a few more minutes. He left after picking some beans and lettuce to accompany his evening meal.

When he approached his garden the following afternoon, hoe in hand and machete on his hip, he had a shock. The kale had once again covered the original cabbage. It also overran one whole row of cabbages and enveloped a third of the frilled carrots. The supposedly dead leaves at the wall had become a sturdy vine, tendrils overtopping the rocks and several arms weaving in the air searching for higher support. "Aah, the pruning efforts to contain this plant haven't worked. It's growing faster than before. I'll have to uproot the whole thing."

At his feet, a rumpled blue-green leaf was leaning toward his boot. He stomped on it without thinking. "Back off! What kind of plant does this?" Mallon smacked it with his hoe.

The kale responded. Its leaves stood straighter, unfurling to their full size and waving back and forth. Disconcerted, he stepped back from the plant and tripped over the mounded row of leeks. Scrambling to his feet, "It must be my imagination—it can't be moving toward me. Oh, yes, it is!" He pulled out his machete and whacked off the closest vines. They writhed and curled into tight spirals. Mallon speared them with the point of the machete and tossed them over the nearest wall.

Overnight the plant and its leaves grew larger, with tougher stems. Daily he hacked the greenery back. He'd started carrying his ax and throwing the leaves over his rock wall onto the hardpan road. Those sprouted and crawled up the wall from the outside. He threw some in the pen with the goats. They took one bite, shuddered, and spat out what they were chewing. They backed away from the pile, and William watched as the leaves wriggled and pushed themselves into the soil.

When he counted his goats the next morning, one was missing, and kale in the pen covered more than half the space. S*uppose? No, plants can't make a goat disappear overnight. He must have been a bolter, but how?*

He went to town and bought weed killer. It might as well have been fertilizer. The kale absorbed it, growing faster and larger after the spraying. Its fierce liveliness made the plant too frightening to eat.

"What do I have to do to stop this malevolent thing? It has covered, no, devoured all the vegetables, and if I didn't know better, I'd say it's headed for my house."

That night Mallon slept restlessly, certain he was hearing the plant creeping closer. In the early morn, he stepped outside and stopped in shock. "Holy mother, it wasn't my imagination. Those leaves can't be more than twenty feet from my door."

He stood in front of his tool shed, hoping for some brilliant insight to stop the plant and save his property and the remnant of his garden. The large can of kerosene caught his eye. *This'll do it in.* The contents sloshed as he carried the can to the closest part of the kale patch. Kale was no longer simply overflowing the small area at the back of the garden. It was a green wave, overrunning and consuming the domesticated vegetables. Mallon drenched the nearest leaves and watched for a reaction.

It was instantaneous. Leaves at his feet turned magenta and spread to their full width. There followed a wave of color pulsing from the closer plants to the far end of the property buried by the kale. The ground vibrated, and William felt a pressure in his chest as if there had been close thunder. At the far end of the kale-covered garden, the plant blackened, and the ebony shade rolled toward him. He threw the rest of the kerosene as far and wide as possible. He backed away from the groping edge of the kale, and whirling around like a discus thrower, sent the empty can spinning to the far end of the field. Leaves curled toward it from all sides and buried it in a mound of green.

William thought to run, but not before he tossed a match on the kerosene-soaked kale. He smiled as the flame soared momentarily. His face fell as the flame faltered, died, and aside from a wisp of smoke, left no evidence of having happened. "What?! Die dreadful plant!"

Once more, he felt as if someone were pressing on his chest. He lurched down the path. He saw the kale had spread across the pen and had the frightened goats cornered. He opened the gate to the goat yard. "OK, boys. You're on your own. Good luck." They nearly knocked him down in their frenzy to abandon the kale-filled pen. Bleating frantically, they scattered downhill and leaped over the low wall adjoining the trail.

"Damn!" He stumbled on the steep rock-strewn path and almost fell. William shouted at the placid faces watching him from the pasture. "Sheep, beware the kale. You get your freedom too." Unmoved, their heads bent again to the grass they were cropping.

At the cove where his small runabout was upturned on the shingle, he righted his boat, pushed it into the shallows, and mounted its outboard motor. He stowed his gas can under the aft seat. With an escape route at hand, William took a moment to look up the slope. "No, that's not possible!" His home was ablaze. A maroon sea of leaves was pulsating around it, spilling over walls and across paddocks. "I…I need to warn someone."

Brilliant purple dazzled his eyes when he managed a last glimpse of his property. "I'll tell George. He saw the first leaves and identified them. He'll understand."

Intent on his heading, William didn't notice the small leaf bit caught in the tread of his shoe.

Previously published in *Kale is a Four-Letter Word*, Patricia Walkow and Chris Allen, eds., Tijeras, NM: Artemesia Publishing, LLC, September 1, 2020, pp. 39-45.

HOW COULD I DISAPPEAR?

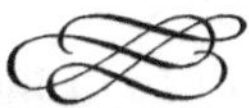

SANDI HOOVER

I'll run away! That was my frequent threat, or promise, to myself. So, I said it again—out loud. "I'll run away!" I thought about running away from home much more as an adult than I ever did as a child.

Daydreams maintained my sanity and became my escape during weeks that sometimes became months when my husband was working overseas. I mused on the law discussed by women whose husbands were out of town—Murphy's Fourth or something. It stated the difficulty of a situation at home would be directly proportional to the distance and problems involved in contacting a husband. This didn't even encompass the day-to-day challenges of raising children and logistics needed to keep a family with only a single adult functioning—barely stably.

Considering throwing it all to the wind and abandoning home and children for freedom occurred on an irregular basis. That idea was frequently stimulated by a combination of small events—the papercuts of daily responsibilities—children's behavior, hormonal fluctuations, and parental and managerial demands, adding up to an overwhelming need to flee.

I was already mentally gone from the lineup of cars dropping children off at school when brake lights on another mother's car just ahead startled me. The squabbling kids, both mine and others', bouncing in the back seat, reached a fever pitch, but I was past reprimanding them.

My turn at the drop-off point. The children were led away to classrooms by adult overseers, and I was freed. Cranking up an oldies station on the radio and rolling the windows down to pretend my tired sedan was a convertible, I didn't fight the steering wheel when the car turned unbidden in a direction unrelated to anything on my day's list. What would happen if the car just kept on going? Somewhat dreamily, I watched city blocks slide past with no sense of *almost there* and the impending need to be galvanized into action. My "to be done today" and shopping lists sat unread and ignored on the passenger seat as I started conjuring places where no one would think to look for me if the car went on and on.

How far could I get? Where would I go? What could I do? Like a person in the Federal Witness Protection Program, or author Erma Bombeck, who said move and leave no forwarding address for children, I plotted places to live where no one would expect to see me. Various locales demanded my attention. I have always loved travel, so liberating my imagination with a mental road trip to free myself was exciting.

Was the other side of town and a room in a cheap motel, or living in a trailer park, far enough away to be lost for as long as I wanted? Probably not, and I started mentally examining the United States map for alternative places to live.

Even though they were as perfect as a non-English speaking foreign country for someone living in southeast Texas, I immediately eliminated the top tier of states in the U.S. They were just too cold to endure, even for escape. It meant I'd have to *live* there, looking and feeling like the Pillsbury doughgirl or the Michelin woman, in layer upon layer of clothes to fend off frostbite. Nope, none of those states was a possible haven.

Moving along, my next area of contemplation and elimination was the southeast. My progressive views would be expressed too soon and were certain to get me killed, or at the very least, noticed. That outcome would not fulfill my goal of hiding and being innocuous.

The northeast was out mostly because of crowded conditions—easy to hide in the throngs, but uncomfortable to live there. And yet once again, it was cold in the winter with snowstorms and shoveling snow, making it miserable for a wimpy person who was chilled when you said, "fifty degrees," much less said, "freezing sleet tonight and blizzard conditions tomorrow." Although New York City was, without question, huge and one could get lost there, I didn't own a wardrobe of black clothes for more than a week, so I would stand out in their monochromatic crowds. Besides, I don't look good in black. Vanity strikes again; another thing moms don't have a chance to develop.

Now where in the rest of the country, and there was still a large portion of the United States to choose from, was I going to vanish? I wanted somewhere large enough the neighbors didn't care who you were or where you went to church or preferably even *if* you went to church.

It couldn't be too near my current home. It needed to be inexpensive because I wasn't going to have a high-paid corporate position to fund my life. Plus, I didn't want to run into an acquaintance accidentally or catastrophe—my family—while grocery shopping.

While worrying over where to go, I thought perhaps the first thing to do was change my appearance. I'd cut my hair really short and dye it purple, get tattoos and work at some big box store. No, it was just too public, and while purple hair was a dramatic difference for me, it wasn't inconspicuous.

Even though my friends were environmentally and socially correct—they said they recycled before it was popular and avoided corporations whose payment policies treated their employees like slaves—I'd bet money they occasionally backslid and shopped in a forbidden store.

Paying everything in cash was going to make it difficult as well. While daydreaming, I tried to avoid thinking about practical things such as new identification and other actual details, but some inserted themselves unasked.

Enough sunshine was a must. My hiding spot needed to be somewhere with a nice climate and interesting scenery. How about a city with a large park or botanic garden? I would hide in plaid flannel and work planting annuals for every change of season. Under a big hat, long sleeves, with gardening gloves, and looking at the ground, I'd never be discovered. I got an instant backache thinking about that vocation, not to mention sore knees and fanny.

Perhaps I could assume a sort of 1940s Veronica Lake look with blonde hair draped over half my face. Hair in my eyes, something I normally hated, and wouldn't wear, would bar recognition from a casual glance. Veronica, in her mid-thirties, wore slinky attire not currently chic. So, I'd opt to wear demure pastel sweater sets with pearls. If I sold perfumes in an upscale boutique in Dallas, I'd never be found.

Kerchoo! Never mind, I forgot about my allergies to strong aromas and whatever many colognes were made of. Since I also didn't own the required sweaters, I'd better think of something else to do.

Well, I had scratched that occupation, but I thought I would like to keep the hair. Maybe I'd find out if blondes really had more fun.

As a teen, I had helped my dad work on our cars. He wanted a boy first, but there I was. Perhaps that was an answer. I'd work in the parts department of a large car dealership in another state. Even though I already spent my days in the car with children, hanging out in a car parts sales area was so far from my current life, it was an unthinkable place for anyone to find me. Not a plant in sight, no greenery, or a breath of fresh air. Argh. Just the thought made me slightly stir crazy. I wanted escape, not purgatory.

New Orleans' charm had always intrigued me. I'd become a redhead and match my Irish temper. Then I'd sit in a garret, a phrase sounding artistically reclusive and poetic, and write florid bodice-ripper novels or dramatic plays where the heroine loves unwisely. Did garrets even exist anymore? How would I find one? More importantly, in New Orleans, were they air-conditioned? Most importantly, what if a hurricane came by? And the odds were good that one would in the foreseeable future. That lovely city is below sea level! Not to mention the pressure of writing.

My mind idling with the engine, I considered and discarded Oklahoma, another state easily reachable from my location. It would be only a day's drive to disappear in rural country there, and the tanned hiker-chick look with sun-streaked blonde hair, rough and ready khaki shorts and boots had great appeal. Hmm, not exactly city attire, but my attitude changed just thinking about the freedom of being out in the open. Could I learn to be useful on a farm? I was quite accustomed to cleaning up after small animals; after all, I had two children, but the possibility of having to slaughter my own dinner made me consider being a vegetarian without even leaving the city.

Eek! No more tornadoes, thank you. I saw one up close. It was extremely impressive, and I never wanted to live in tornado alley after watching transformers on power poles flash with brilliant blue and shocking red before going dark inside the oncoming funnel. Hiding in a bathtub with a mattress over me held no appeal. Especially if all I could live in was a trailer. I'm convinced they are tornado magnets.

Clearly, northern Texas, Oklahoma, and those flat rectangular states were out of the question. Calm weather was high on the list of my necessities after growing up with earthquakes in California as a child and living with hurricanes in Houston as an adult.

So, the possibilities were getting slimmer. No snow, no tornadoes, no hurricanes; I was getting pretty picky about the location. I needed a place large enough not to become the object of interest as the new person in town, but still, I wanted to find a niche.

If I hid in a big city like Los Angeles, where any extreme was standard, a severe black hairdo, with fishnet stockings, plus a rerun on platform shoes with a short skirt could work and had a retro appeal. On second thought, it had been too long since I wore those clothes with the English mod look of the time. Although retrieving both youth and the freedom of childlessness were attractive, the desperate appearance of someone hoping to recapture a lost era was not who I wanted to be.

Time for an assessment of what I thought might work. Okay, wearing casual clothes, having blonde hair, and some way to make a living out in the open was settled. Lots of negatives in location, not many positives yet. Where was I to go?

How about some territory where I could leave my hair straight, grow it long, and wear it in braids like Willie Nelson? I'd add denim, put on a bandana and hairnet, and work in a school cafeteria in a large town.

Great heavens no, what an awful idea. Was that prompted by some country and western song I just subconsciously heard on the radio? The object was to *avoid* children, not be subjected to even more of them. Of course, being completely opposite of any expectation of something I would do, it might work. But emphatically, no! It was painful to even think about standing surrounded by noisy children with low blood sugar or, alternatively, a sugar high.

That outfit, without the hairnet, and with a blouse showing my décolleté could possibly work elsewhere. What about a rural biker bar? Those were prevalent in east Texas piney woods where no one would expect me, but the aroma of stale beer, loud music, and burly ruffians covered in tattoos didn't appeal for even one second. That idea was conceived, envisioned, and discarded in a shudder of relief. Sigh, I wasn't getting very far in making an escape decision.

Driving through the green tunnels of Houston's streets stimulated pictures of northern California and the immense trees living there. The image following those trees was of the cold fog, rain, and gloom essential to growing something gigantic. As the sun-loving woman I am, no way could I be happy living in that environment. Those hiking shorts and boots I was imagining left lots of space in between for goosebumps—another large sigh of regret. As much as I loved visiting there, as a permanent location for me, a dreary climate wasn't going to happen. Trading one form of depression for another was no answer.

While coastal Oregon is the same as northern California, only more so, inland it is quite desert-like since the coast range blocks rain. Aha, that meant a bearable number of cloudy days. Interior Oregon seemed like a possibility, and it was a progressive state with laws to protect human rights. Okay, what about a frizzy 'fro, to go with long skirts and loose gauze blouses with lots of beads? A bit of an unrepentant hippie, this was so similar to my standard self it wasn't camouflage. And too, there was still the colder winter and hotter summer climate by virtue of location to contend with. Heavens, it was difficult to find the ideal place and persona to disappear into.

I looked south. Perhaps Arizona. It has always been a state with lots of sun, and warm, no, make that searingly hot, days. The compensation was the charming, almost human, Saguaros, and the mountains were elegantly exposed, a delight for a person with geological training.

Parts of the state held appeal, my favorite town being Sedona. However, the cost of living there was too high, and not only was it small enough to have to tell one's story and keep track of what had been said, but it also had a significant snow season. I still was spoiled, thinking I wouldn't live where I had to shovel the white stuff.

So going further south, Tucson was entrancing with its Spanish and Mexican flair. Best, it had no snow, but at the other end of seasons, the number of days over one hundred degrees was frightening. Bad idea after all, and Phoenix was turning into a hotter Los Angeles, without the ocean at hand. Scratch Arizona.

I even considered Mexico, but the complications of language and nationality overwhelmed my imagination as I considered a quick getaway. If only I had taken Spanish instead of German in high school.

I got this far in my thinking more than once but never could decide on the perfect international or U.S. location. This inability to settle on a hideout saved me from making a column headline—*Unfit Mother Abandons Children.* Or across the entire page—*Mother Disappears, Father and Children Distraught*—with a heartrending photo of sobbing children clinging to their father.

Usually, I had driven to the Houston City Limit sign by then and was startled to see open rice fields looming ahead and buildings diminishing in the rear-view mirror. And at that point, I wondered, what the kids were doing in school? Were they behaving? Wasn't it almost time for recess…were they having a good time with friends? I could imagine laughter and smiling faces. No way could I miss the next installment in their young lives.

I pulled into a gas station parking lot, with Brubeck's *Take Five* on the radio—absolutely right on target. I snapped back to the present and realized with just a few more deep breaths, I could cope with a day's normal duties: my imagined freedom—sanity-saving. Being a grownup isn't always easy.

I filled up the car for the week ahead and thought about the chauffeur license I didn't have, although it was an important job I fulfilled. One of my responsibilities was getting dancers to class and soccer players to games. Those weekly routes had become so routine I was a moving map of the city.

The adult benefit of handling carpool was open time after children were busy with their games and classes. *Then* there was the opportunity to talk with other mothers who faced the same things. Comparing notes made us laugh and kept us sane. We were a sisterhood of women coping with life and creating bright, curious children.

The trip back toward town flashed by as I reviewed my various selves. Oh well, they would probably be boring in short order. I discarded them one by one. First to go was Ms. Goth. I wasn't very fond of her, and black hair wasn't flattering to me anyway. Next on my list of abandoned personas was Miss Prim, the fragrance saleswoman. I would have had a hard time maintaining that level of decorum. It wasn't difficult to leave her behind.

My gardener in the big hat and the hiker chick were really variations on a theme. Off they went together, hopefully to some bright green space where they could lie on their backs in warm sunshine and discuss the merits of native plant species.

Ahh, lastly, the redhead in the garret. No need to be a non-operatic version of Mimi and die in my impoverished hovel, but writing still had appeal. It offered an adult outlet I could indulge in after all were asleep, but a garret sounded claustrophobic and confining. Keeping a journal and throwing away the fear of hurricanes, I could salvage some of her.

Time to face life. Picking up my list at my first stop, I added a lined notebook to it and headed for the grocery store but veered off when I saw a beauty salon sign saying *Walk-ins Welcome*. How much, I wondered, would it cost to become a blonde?

Previously published as "Running Away From Home," *Currents: Corrales Writing Group 2015 Anthology*, Patricia Walkow, ed., North Charleston, SC: CreateSpace, October 4, 2015, pp. 231-236.

BUT WHAT IF THE BUDDHISTS GOT IT WRONG?

JIM TRITTEN

Having approached the stage in life where the end is in sight, it is fitting for me to contemplate what happens next. The end has already arrived for an ever-increasing number of my friends and family members. A good friend's mother asked him just before she passed, "Is that all there is?"

I had figured out what I wanted to believe many years ago. There are three major theories of what happens after we take our last breath.[1] These theories shape and influence how we live our lives. Having now lived most of my life, I am going to review the question "Is that all there is?" once more and see if these theories make any more sense today. What can I expect after I have taken my last breath?

I have the impression that all Abrahamic faiths[2], such as Islam, Christianity, and Judaism, tell us we will go to a specific place upon death. The place depends upon how we acted during our lifetime and the particular religion we accept. Each of these religions generally tells us God will judge us but doesn't share his criterion.

Some religions tell us the depth of our faith determines the life that we live. Many practitioners believe their deeds on earth can influence

God's judgment. Some believers spend a lifetime trying to work their way into a rewarding afterlife. However, Paul, the Apostle, tells us that deeds alone are not the way to find salvation.[3] Other religions tell us explicit acts can be a ticket to a pleasing hereafter.

Despite differences that have often led to violence, most Muslims, Christians, and Jews (with some caveats) appear to accept they only get one shot at life. Each of them offers some promise of an afterlife experience directly attributable to their faith and/or their actions on earth. There are slight variations in the Jewish faith and with the Catholic Purgatory as neither heaven nor hell. Still, only one human experience on earth.

It seems to me the Dharmic religions[4], on the other hand, such as Hinduism, Buddhism, Sikhism, and Jainism, envisage a more continued existence with the actions of the individual determining the next stage of life. Essentially these religions seem to espouse reforming, hopefully upward, until the believer attains a final perfect existence on earth. Once perfection is achieved, entry is granted to the Otherworld—presumably, a heaven with a fulfilling and rewarding afterlife.

The key difference appears to be if you do not get your behavior into the perfection category during one episode in a long repeating life cycle, you get another opportunity to get it right the next time. A Dharmic believer achieves perfection when he or she has no more earthly cravings for experiences or possessions. Said another way, these believers are doomed to remain on this imperfect earth plane until they figure out what it will take to escape. Moreover, if they don't get it right, they may come back as a camel to live life again on earth and learn some lesson or make up for some bad karma.

There is a third major view of what happens after life. Atheists/agnostics/humanists are generally convinced that once we have exhaled our last breath, nothing follows. What constitutes our body is returned to the earth where some new organism uses recycled elements[5]. Pretty straightforward. It's over when it's over. No rewards. No punishment.

How do these different views manifest themselves into a real-world decision about what code should guide us during our life on this earth? On the one hand, if we assume life is a one-shot deal, then should we experience all there is? Or do we consciously abstain from material pleasures because of the promise of a reward or reckoning in the afterlife? On the other hand, if we have multiple existences, then do we pace our experiences knowing if necessary, we can do it or get it right next time? If we accept the Dharmic view, then it might be easier to accept unhappiness in this lifetime with the explanation we are paying for some karmic past transgression and that this too will pass.

In the Dharmic view, if perfection is only achieved when there are no more earthly cravings for experiences or possessions, what do we see by observing Dharmic holy men? In my mind, I conjure up pictures of men wrapped in a sheet with a headpiece and sandals. My image is of holy men of poverty without worldly goods to signify their status.

Similarly, if we look at the holy men of the Abrahamic tradition, I personally first think of the Bishop of Rome, Vicar of Jesus Christ, Successor of the Prince of the Apostles, Supreme Pontiff of the Universal Church, Primate of Italy, Archbishop and Metropolitan of the Roman Province, Sovereign of the State of Vatican City, Servant of the Servants of God[6]. He is known as the Pope. He hardly lives in poverty and carries a history of organizational intolerance that includes the Inquisition of days past. Other Abrahamic religions embrace similar fanaticism even today.

The New Testament of the Bible tells us not to eschew an abundant life. According to the scripture, after having attained abundance, an individual can do good deeds and then share their good fortune with others[7]. Sounds similar to other New Testament discussions about a believer's ability to do good deeds because they have previously been selected for salvation[8]. I learned about predestination as a teenager when I studied for the God and Country Award. Only later did I realize that was not a ticket for unfettered behavior and salvation regardless.

With all of this conflicting advice and behavior, who has the moral high ground? There is a great deal of respect for the bully pulpit of both the Pope and the Dalai Lama. If man has a free choice in his spiritual beliefs, does any single path provide a clear answer to how we should live? Option one—one shot at life with just desserts when it is over? Option two—multiple existences, each with an opportunity to achieve perfection or pay for past transgressions? Or, option three, do the atheists/agnostics/humanists have it right, and there are no afterlife consequences or rewards?

Does behavior on earth depend upon what we believe about an afterlife? Is this philosophical distinction relegated to the inner-most reaches of our brains to be filed away with much of the discussion we had while growing up and attending school? Or does it have any applicability to actual events we might expect to face in a typical lifetime?

One example of direct relevancy in everyone's future is how to decide on ending the life of a loved one. Assume we are in the role of agent, surrogate, or guardian[9] over another individual's health care decisions. Do our core beliefs about an afterlife shape how that decision will be made?[10]

An individual raised or schooled in traditional Abrahamic religions might view making a decision on ending all life of another human based upon a desire to stop pain and ease misery. Survivors often discuss the departed as having finally been relieved from their suffering. If the decision-maker accepts a single birth and an afterlife based upon one's spiritual beliefs, passing may lead the dying to a better place. Obituaries frequently mention the departed as having gone to their reward in heaven.

Most Western governments act as if they accept when someone dies, that is all there is—the atheist/agnostic/humanist view. Alternatively, if the government takes the life of a condemned prisoner, perhaps they think they are hastening the delivery of an individual to a place where they will suffer for eternity. I suppose there have been cases when governments act to end the life of someone; they do so envisaging delivery to heaven.

An individual with Dharmic beliefs is likely to view the inability to sustain physical life as a marker in the soul's passage from one existence to another. When a Dalai Lama passes on, his followers launch a search for the reincarnated soul in another body. Sometimes secular governments get involved with selecting a new spiritual leader who inherits the mantle from the recently departed. Dharmic religions feature multiple births with multiple passings to a new life still on the path to perfection.

Do any of these types of belief systems make end-of-life decisions easier? It would seem to me a decision-maker might find it easier to make an end-of-life decision if the individual would be relieved of suffering, be guaranteed a life-after-death in heaven, and know the individual will pass on to a new existence where they get another shot at it? Or perhaps the guilty bastard deserves death, and a state-ordered execution is a way to hasten their journey? Most end-of-life decisions involve many of these justifications. The dying will (1) either end their life, and there is nothing else. Or (2) the passing will be rewarded or on the path to perfection. Or (3) death is a path to deserved eternal damnation.

Whichever way satisfies one's inner quest for the meaning of life and what happens after life is probably the correct answer—as long as the path is chosen by the individual and not forced upon the unwilling.

My own choice is to lead a life that does not embarrass me or those close to me. To do good things for others without any expectation of a reward. To behave in a manner that would preclude examination on the front page of *The Washington Post.* To assume that I will either find a reward or a path to a reward or absolutely nothing upon reaching the end of my life. I have lived my life in a manner that has been equally shaped by my early religious upbringing, a secular atheist/agnostic/humanist education, and the culture of our society.

But, just in case the Buddhists got it wrong, and we only go through life once, I'll also keep hammering away at these modest interim objectives: drive an Aston Martin AM-RB 001 along the Pacific Coast Highway between Carmel and Big Sur, California, sip Glenlivet 50-Year-Old Single Malt Scotch Whisky while in the Green Room of Castle Fraser, wear an Armani suit to the ceremony where I receive the Nobel Prize, fly a jet upside down over Mount Vesuvius, pair a gourmet dinner at Noma with Chateau Cheval Blanc 1943, sleep on a Hästens mattress at the Vivanta hotel in Taj-Bekal, India, smoke only E.P. Carrillo Encore Majestic cigars while gambling on *Le Laperouse*, and eat bacon like there's no tomorrow. Just in case.[11]

Previously published in *SouthWest Writers 2019 Winners Anthology: Annual Writing Contest*, Albuquerque, NM, SouthWest Writers, September 4, 2019, pp.88-93. The chapter was awarded a Gold Medal for First Place, 2019 Annual Writing Contest, SouthWest Writers —Philosophy.

NOTES

4. BUT WHAT IF THE BUDDHISTS GOT IT WRONG?

1. Francis X. Clooney, SJ, "One-Birth, Many-Births: A Conversation Reborn A Response to 'Perspectives on Reincarnation: Hindu, Christian, and Scientific,' a Thematic Issue of *Religions*," *Religions 2018*, 9, 204, 2 July 2018. https://www.mdpi.com/2077-1444/9/7/204/htm
2. http://www.newworldencyclopedia.org/entry/Abrahamic_religions
3. Ephesians 2:9 as cited in https://biblehub.com/ephesians/2-9.htm
4. http://aumamen.com/question/what-are-the-differences-between-abrahamic-eastern-religions
5. http://atheistfoundation.org.au/article/atheists-perspective-death/, http://www.chicagonow.com/an-atheist-in-illinois/2017/03/an-agnostic-approach-to-religions-and-the-afterlife/, and https://www.thelancet.com/journals/lancet/article/PIIS0140-6736(05)67486-7/fulltext
6. https://www.britannica.com/topic/pope
7. https://www.christianitytoday.com/edstetzer/2015/march/what-does-it-mean-to-have-abundant-life.html
8. https://www.bibleref.com/Ephesians/2/Ephesians-2-9.html
9. New Mexico Uniform Health Care Decisions Act, 24-7A-1. Definitions. https://hscethics.unm.edu/common/pdf/uniform-healthcare-decisions-act.pdf
10. Susan M. Setta and Sam D. Shemie, "An explanation and analysis of how world religions formulate their ethical decisions on withdrawing treatment and determining death," *Philosophy, Ethics, and Humanities in Medicine*, 2015; 10: 6. https://ncbi.nlm.nih.gov/pmc/articles/PMC4396881 Published online 2015 Mar 11.
11. The author would like to thank Charles A. Meconis, Ph.D., formerly Father Charles Meconis, and Pastor Mark A. Mayerstein, MDiv, for their critique and suggestions.

THERE'S A DIVA IN THE HOUSE

SANDI HOOVER

My husband and I grew up hearing and loving opera classics like Aida, Tosca, and Carmen. We enjoy attending live performances whenever possible. Years ago, while living in Houston, we were thrilled by the artistry of the local opera company and became enthusiastic supporters.

Friends cheerfully shared tales of their housing a visiting singer. When an opportunity arose to host a soprano brought to town for a performance, we thought it would be a nice way to extend our support for an opera company we enjoyed. We had a spare bedroom and bath since our children were grown and gone, a living room with a piano, and are relatively easy to live with—why not offer to help? Reportedly Donald Rumsfeld once said, "You don't know what you don't know," about a new situation. We weren't even sure what that meant, but we found out!

As donors to the opera, we had lunched with Madame X, a blonde *Brunhilde* from New York, two years before, so she was not a totally unknown quantity. But a lunch, however lengthy, is not the same as sharing your living space with someone you've actually barely met.

Well, we thought innocently, it would probably be a couple, perhaps three, weeks.

After telling the Artistic Manager we would love to host Madame X, our first surprise was finding out her required rehearsals plus the performances would be just two days less than a month—and that was a month with thirty-one days. OK, just a bit longer than expected and arriving a bit earlier than we had thought she might, but no problem—mostly.

We swiftly changed our return reservations on a long-planned trip and arrived home the day before our guest appeared with two large suitcases in a car loaned by another supporter. On her second trip from the car, she carried several shopping bags full of provisions she picked up at the grocery store on the way from the airport. "Just a few things since I prefer not to eat with the cast. They tend to frequent places I don't like."

Oops, different feeding habits hadn't occurred to us since we are uncomplaining omnivores. If it doesn't attack us first, we'll eat it. Surprised but instantly recovering, we scrambled to rearrange storage space in the kitchen.

Designated shelf and vegetable bin space were immediately cleared in the refrigerator for almond milk, yogurt, sprouted pumpkin seeds, free-range eggs, amaranth, dried seaweed, and a myriad of other necessities. A shelf in the pantry was swept clean of our foods and re-filled with her variety of boxes of flax and oatmeal, bags of nuts, trail mixes, protein powders, chamomile, and throat soothing teas, plus sweeteners and coffee.

It was lovely she wanted to provide for her own special needs, but it felt frighteningly like the holidays when all possible places containing food were crammed to overflowing. You hoped nothing in the back got forgotten and was remembered only when purple fuzz was seen creeping out of bulging containers.

"We were just about to have lunch. Would you like a turkey sandwich also?" I asked as she returned to the kitchen. "No thanks, I am eating gluten-free," was Madame X's reply. Who knew? Why hadn't I thought to ask that sort of question when we offered to host? So I proffered a turkey and cheese rollup in lettuce instead. We all enjoyed a brief lunch. Then she went off to unpack.

Our "guest suite" was quite simple—merely a cheerful average-sized bedroom with expansive windows opening to the wildflower-filled grassy area we call our backyard. Dense azalea bushes provide green privacy both by the windows and at the back fence. The bedroom had an attached bathroom, but essentially, modest was an accurate assessment. I imagine many minimum-security prisons offer more space and luxurious amenities for their white-collar prisoners.

Although the room is not overlarge, I hoped she would find a welcoming haven in the queen-size bed, with its top-of-the-line Tempur-Pedic mattress, freshly made with colorful sheets, and topped by a homey quilt with matching pillows. So much for my high expectations. The bed wasn't mentioned, probably not even noticed, as it was instantly covered with an explosion of pants, dresses, and tops. Bureau drawers were filled, and suitcases were emptied then relegated to the garage, hauled there by my compliant husband. Counter surfaces in both bedroom and bath filled rapidly with all manner of *accoutrements,* including makeup, makeup removers, creams, hairspray, hot curlers, dryers, and other feminine necessities—most of them clashingly fragrant.

It was late fall, and the weather was chilly. The cold didn't stop us from tossing on sweaters and opening doors and windows the minute she left the house in order to reduce the aromatic density of her perfumes.

The bathroom had been scrubbed to a high shine for her arrival. And arrival time was the last time it was either clean or pristine. I was reminded of the way our wild backyard birds take baths—lots of frantic activity and much ado about moving water around—but hardly a drop on their feathers. With birds, more water is flung than is absorbed. Although it wasn't intentional, there was no way to avoid hearing all the splashing water noises, and I wondered if it was the same in her bathing. It's amazing how far and wide soapsuds can be spread.

Madame X was given a key to the house, a garage door opener, and a place to park the car outside—a place allowing an easy turnaround for exiting. Over time, we gathered it was important since her loaned car collected an increasing number of scrapes and dings during the month. Many New Yorkers don't drive often; obviously, she was one who always took public transportation or walked. Houston traffic is not the place for the faint of heart or a novice driver!

The owner of the car said after her departure, "She evidently stopped by running into something." With that in mind, it was fortuitous she didn't park in our garage. The broken limbs on the azaleas flanking the driveway weren't a concern; they benefit from pruning anyway.

Music is frequent entertainment in our home with a wide selection of styles on CD, so we are accustomed to melodies emanating from wall speakers in many rooms. Plus, my husband is a serious pianist and practices often, usually daily, for more than an hour. Too often, the time he anticipated practicing coincided with her required vocal exercises at the piano.

We soon discovered there is a significant difference between the opera music we normally heard and a soprano tuning up. Arias can be lively, emotionally wrought, solemn, or sweetly full of love. Warm-up phrases are none of those. Guess what? There is no volume control button either. Professional singers, either trained or created by birth, are designed to project to the auditorium's back wall. The back wall of an auditorium was much farther away than our living room wall was. Piercing might be a good term.

Our very contemporary house had an open floor plan, and sound always carried well, all too well in this case. There were not enough doors to close to muffle the sound of tuning vocal cords for an hour and a half every day before departure to the concert venue for rehearsals.

Our cat dove under the bed the moment her vocal practice started. Once I lay on the floor and stuck my head under the bed, hoping our kitty had found the answer. Nope, it wasn't any better than hiding in the farthest reaches of the house. I put on headphones and CDs and created many reasons to leave home.

Yet another thing we didn't know—singers' throats need humidity. How much? Even in Houston, we considered forty percent humid enough to complain about it being soggy and turn on an air conditioner. We didn't know soggy! I tiptoed into her room with a load of clean towels and needed gills. The walls in the bedroom were dripping with moisture, and weren't they starting to turn a strange shade of green from the humidifier we loaned her? The windows were running with so much condensation the backyard was invisible. When we measured it, the humidity in her suite was over seventy percent! The carpet was so damp I heard it squish, looked down, and could swear I saw water puddling at my feet!

Evidently, that wasn't enough humidity for her throat.

Lengthy, no, make that really, really, really long, daily showers were accompanied by strange gurgling noises and various warm-up exercises. Even in Houston, we tried to conserve water. It's surprising, but water shortages are a problem there too. In trying not to be obviously personally critical, I mentioned it to her while ostentatiously carrying only slightly used water outside to pour on patio pots. She didn't see it applying to her. The showers and sloshing baths continued as usual.

Madame X was lovely and dramatically beautiful when artfully wearing stage makeup—the final step in her long bathing ritual, along with lots of perfume. When time allowed her to stop and spend a few minutes with us, her curiosity about cultural differences between New

Yorkers and transplanted Texans generated lively conversations. We also got some entertaining insiders' stories of professional singers and the arts in general.

Timing was always fluctuating since rehearsal schedules seemed to change daily. Having her personal entrance and the key was essential for her comings and goings without being dependent on our being awake. She frequently came in after midnight. That erratic nature of sleep reflected itself in her highly variable awaking and meal times. The easy answer was all of us quite happily just doing our own thing and not planning to share meals. It was akin to having an older teenager in the house, picking through the items in the refrigerator for whatever appealed at the moment, regardless of the standard meal expectation.

One special time, however, we did dine together. She generously offered to cook a typical northern Italian meal, such as she had loved while growing up. Then we understood why she was shaped like the stereotypical Valkyrie. An antipasto plate for starters, then *soupe crasse*, a cheese-and-bread soup, anchovies in green sauce with *brasato di vitello* (a special braised veal), and *torta di Sant'Antonio* for dessert (a red wine, cinnamon, apple tart). It was delicious and very out of the ordinary!

It also demanded the use of every pan, bowl, measuring cup, and stirring spoon in the kitchen. A sumptuous feast, it was well worth our scrubbing down counters, cook surfaces, and all the containers and utensils for the treat of her gourmet meal.

She said making and taking her lunches and dinners helped stretch her limited funds. When the time came to provide the requisite gifts for the cast, Madame X decided making hers would be another way to conserve dollars. Homemade chocolate truffles were her forte, so she invested in great quality chocolate, special cocoa powder, gourmet cinnamon, and European-style butter. She also bought little gift boxes, liners, and tissues. Mentally adding the cost of the purchases, I was sure she would have saved money by buying commercially made truffles.

We emptied more shelves in the refrigerator to hold cookie sheets, finally containing hundreds of chocolate balls with varied ingredients. Some of the cast were allergic to nuts, others were not eating dairy products, and still others were getting classic truffles. Nobody just eats a meal anymore.

The entire selection of mixing bowls and measuring spoons made a repeat performance, along with plastic wrap on the counters, bowls in which to dredge the truffles with cocoa, and plates to hold them temporarily. The kitchen was unavailable during three days of frenetic activity when she was not at rehearsals. Between melting chocolate, mixing with butter, forming the balls with flavorings, chilling the first step, rolling in dusty cocoa to coat them, and organizing by flavors and ingredients, any other use of the kitchen and counter space for meal preparation vanished.

We ate out.

Like splashed water and soapsuds, it is remarkable how far both melted chocolate and cocoa dust can spread. Those browns blended into the pattern on our granite counters so well they disappeared for a while. We almost believed in the spontaneous generation of chocolate as little chocolate leftovers appeared for weeks afterward.

Days and rehearsals passed; we grew accustomed to the various sounds of practice. We found many reasons to be out of the house for the most part of tuning up, and some semblance of a routine developed. Halfway through it, the month seemed infinitely long when we looked ahead. But time actually moved at its normal rate, and her stay came to an end.

Who knows whether it was her chocolate truffles or simply the chemistry of the personnel. The cast was happy, our diva sang well, and the opera was a terrific success.

We learned a lot—about our tolerance for change, about differences in perspectives, and about asking many more questions before blithely volunteering to share your home with a stranger.

Previously published in *Currents: Corrales Writing Group 2015 Anthology*, Patricia Walkow, ed., North Charleston, SC: CreateSpace, October 4, 2015, pp. 33-39.

SAUNAGUS

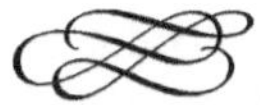

JIM TRITTEN

Perspiration rained down my face, burning my eyes as though bathed in acid. The saltiness reminded me of tumbling through ocean waves when I was a kid. Internal pressures forced my mouth open while my stomach retched. Starving for oxyge*n*, I inhaled a bushel of oppressive superheated air. My lungs rejected the intake. I coughed and grimaced when bile seared my throat and rose into my nasal passages. I leaned back to stabilize and closed my eyes. My hands found the smooth wooden seat. Involuntary spasms followed as my palms and fingertips blistered.

The shock stopped my heart. I felt the cold water before my mind registered what was happening. I opened my eyes wide, gasped, and took in another lungful of air while I reacted to the frigid water drenching my near-naked body. I roared at the top of my lungs, invoking the name of our Lord and begging for a quick death. I shuddered and collapsed in on myself as the icy freshwater replaced the sweat that soaked the towel cushioning my bony rear end. My mouth gaped open seeking oxygen. I inhaled an even larger mass of still-superheated air. The cooling water evaporated in the heat, and I felt myself loosen up. I wiped the refreshing liquid from my face, reveled in the rapid change of skin temperature, and opened my still-stinging eyes to see a shadowy figure with a pail retreat through the open door. I looked up and reflected on what the hell I was doing in that wooden-planked room.

~

A *saunagus* (sauna goose) is a Nordic term describing a particular type of sauna treatment performed in Denmark. My Danish wife Jasmine and I were staying at a prestigious *kurhotel* that offered numerous opportunities to improve one's health. *Saunagus* boldly purports to detox your body, boost your blood circulation, revitalize your immune system, and give you a gigantic energy kick. It is mist therapy with a water/essential oils mixture ladled on hot stones.

I'd been in saunas in the U.S. before, and at times, some participants poured water on the heated stones, gently dripping small amounts of water from a ladle on stones causing a sizzling sound, steam to form, and the humidity to rise a bit. The effect was to make the room seem hotter, but I survived this before. So, what could hurt by adding some natural oils to some steam?

The answer is Leo, our *saunagus* dominatrix from Finland. Petite and soft-spoken, how could we know she would throw a bucket of ice-cold water on our hot pink bodies? She seemed like such a nice girl. Perhaps our Danish hosts outsource anything that might upset the guests? Leo wore a black dress-like gym outfit seemingly totally inappropriate for the setting. Must be the uniform for *gusmeisters*.

And, of course, Leo was nice. She came back into the sauna *sans* bucket, bearing a glass bowl filled with a dark golden liquid. She smiled, asking if we found the cold water refreshing. We lied. "Yes, Leo." After nearly killing us, yes, it was refreshing. I guess that's only half a lie.

Leo passed around the basin after demonstrating how to scoop the thick golden liquid and rub it all over our exposed skin. Pure, raw monofloral honey made from organically-raised bees, she explained. Imported from New Zealand—and I thought they only raised sheep. I cheated and put my finger in my mouth. Delicious. I rubbed honey all over, including into my thinning hair. I kept my eyes closed lest rivulets of the nectar upset the delicate balance of fluids guarding my corneas. As our bodies responded to the heat, sweet whiffs from the honey stimulated our olfactory receptors. Jasmine rubbed it soothingly all over my back. I smiled even while my skin temperature rose, and I remembered it was Jasmine's idea to experience a *saunagus*. I'm a Navy carrier pilot, after all. We rise to any challenge.

Leo smirked as she explained the maximum temperature in the sauna would reach ninety degrees Celsius. My brain melted when I tried to make the conversion to Fahrenheit.

The door opened and closed, letting in some cool outside air. It took a minute for me to realize she departed. In the romantic candlelight, I looked around at the dozen or so fellow scantily-clad travelers on this journey of discovery. Leo was Finnish, everyone else other than me was Danish, and Leo delivered her explanations in English. Nordic people are very polite. They smile a lot.

The cool air signaled Leo's return with what appeared to be branches from a bush in her hands. "Bend over," the *Marquisa* de Sade commanded. Whack—Leo brought the branches down on my neighbor's back. Whack, whack, whack. She hit him three times in rapid succession. He thanked her. He thanked her? For beating him with a switch? I wondered if I might make a discreet exit without embarrassing myself or my Danish wife.

"Your turn. Aspen branches." *I hope they're organic.*

I offered my back with thoughts of the cat 'o nine tails flaying raw an errant seaman's back in the good old days of rocks and shoals—U.S. Navy discipline from the age of sail, before civilization set in. Whack. It didn't hurt. Whack, whack, whack. The room now smelled of the outdoors. Like walking through the crisp aroma of a Nordic forest. I thanked Leo (*why did I do that?)* and silently thought of telling Jasmine what I thought of her idea when we were alone later.

After beating everyone, Leo let in more cool air when she departed, but it didn't take long before sweat poured from our bodies again. And I sat on the lowest level—the coolest part of the sauna. I learned to tilt my head just so and watch the perspiration and honey drip from the same spot at the end of my nose to form a sweet puddle on the wooden plank between my feet. Drip. Drip, Drip. I dared not move my feet lest the soles burn on the wood. Perhaps this would be the time to go into a meditation and zone out for a while.

The monkey brain refused to quiet, and thoughts raced through my head. Why in God's name did I agree to Jasmine's suggestion? Shouldn't I have taken it as an omen when I signed a four-page disclaimer absolving the *kurhotel* of any responsibilities? And filled out an equally long checklist of all known ailments?

The door opened, and Leo the Lioness came in with multiple buckets. She offered them to all of us after demonstrating what to do with them. Place the bucket of cold water above your head and dump the contents. Ice cubes spilled out with the liquid, clinking as they landed on the hardwood floor, shrinking as they melted. I don't think this time my heart stopped. Maybe I got used to it, or perhaps it's different if you do it yourself. I wiped the cool liquid from my body and swim trunks and rubbed it on my head. Leo left the sauna—pails, hips, and gym dress swinging as she departed in search of some new torment.

Returning with a small wooden bowl filled with white crystals, she explained "Icelandic sea salt" while she demonstrated how to rub the mineral on our skin. "Rub harder—you need to clean out those pores." My skin turned a rosy pink under the crystalline scrub. Leo ducked out, this time returning with a wooden pail and ladle. The heat rose after she closed the door.

Leo took her time to explain how our pores were now open, our bodies ready to receive a healing treatment of oil-infused steam. I wondered which oils she planned to use, but at this point, she lapsed into Danish. *Is she explaining the next torture in Danish because she is afraid it might send me bolting for the exit?* I like the perfumes from essential oils. We use an atomizer in our house and favor star anise to mask the odors from four cat boxes.

She added oils into the bucket and ladled drips on the hot stones of the sauna. The effect? Delightful. Pleasant fragrances tickled our noses and induced a calm usually only present during meditation. I jostled my body to ensure every pore received this gift so it might do its magic. I vaguely sensed the cool air as Leo left the sauna. My perspiration increased, washing off the sea salt, forming white crystalline puddles on the planked floorboards.

I closed my eyes and imagined floating in a sensory deprivation tank. Detached from reality with heavenly scents healing my lungs. I even forgot about "thanking" Jasmine later. I was balanced between the air and the sea, with every pore absorbing life-giving energies. Pure bliss.

A chill interrupted this dream. Leo appeared in the doorway. I swear she wore a fascist armband and jackboots. "Show me your backs," she ordered. *Sieg Heil!* I slunk forward and was rewarded by four whacks on my shoulders. This time they hurt. Before I could figure out if she had switched from aspen branches to a rose bush, she yelled something Danish, and we all hustled out of the sauna. Outside, Jasmine and my fellow travelers told me to put on a robe and flip-flops. We were going to jump into the sea. *I'm a Navy pilot, not a SEAL.*

Technically the *Øresund* is not the open ocean. It is the waters between Denmark and Sweden. You can see the opposite shore from the beach. I've never swum in the *Øresund* but have observed nude bathers near my mother-in-law's apartment as they immersed and then quickly erupted from the water a little bit bluer than when they started.

Our little band of heated and beaten health seekers walked through the spa to the far corner exit. I saw the knowing grins and smirks on other clients—they knew our fate. I noted Leo was absent. Had she gone off to release the sharks for our swim? A frigid, icy gale howled while we went along an asphalt walkway to the road crossing, waited until the rural rush of small cars and cyclists subsided, then went down a coastal sand path to a wooden jetty.

By the time I reached the pier, I could no longer feel my limbs or nose. I watched in horror as all the Danes took off their robes, exposing their lily-white legs and ruddy backs to what had to be the coldest gale I ever felt, counting when I attended Arctic survival training in the Navy. Each Dane, including my Viking wife Jasmine, went down the ladder at the end of the jetty and into the water. I grimaced when they all ducked their heads under the surface. *Egad!* I was not going under the cold water. I wrapped my robe tighter around my body.

The Danes all beckoned me into the *Øresund*, and I realized if I did not join them, there would be a lot of embarrassment later with the family. I'm a fearless pilot, right? So, without further hesitation, I threw my robe on the railing, put my flip-flops on the deck, and climbed down the ladder. Slowly. Actually, I only slowed when the water level reached my swim trunks. I thought of the 1994 *Seinfeld* television episode "The Hamptons," where the character George Costanza tries to explain to Jerry Seinfeld's girlfriend about penile shrinkage.

As the ice-cold *Øresund* hit my chest, I released my hold on the ladder, casting adrift into the open ocean. I again broke the Third Commandment and, presuming hell would at least take off the chill, wished for an early death. There is no comparison to any other cold I ever experienced in my entire life. I know my heart stopped for at least a minute. My conscious brain refused to function—eyes couldn't focus. I heard nothing. Mr. Freeze's (*Batman & Robin*, 1997) cold gun couldn't have been more effective. My jaw started chattering on its own. I did my best to keep my tongue from sliding between teeth tapping a staccato rhythm. I regained some semblance of time and place. Then I remembered one more thing. I ducked my head under the water.

A mid-May *Øresund* bath was just what I needed to wash out any residual raw monofloral New Zealand honey and Icelandic sea salt crystals from my hair. And as an added side benefit, I was now ready to be packed away for trans-Atlantic shipment in sub-zero steerage class.

I rose from the depths of the sea reborn and in a frantic search for the ladder. “No, you must go up the other ladder,” Jasmine yelled from about ten feet away. I shuffled my feet along the stony bottom, spitting out *Øresund* water. I was the last of our group to climb the ladder back into the cold wind that tased my body into further surrender. *Thank you, Jasmine. You owe me big time.*

I have no recollection of walking back along the beach, crossing the street, and then back up the path to the *kurhotel*. As we got to the spa entry, one of the men tapped me on the shoulder and said, “You’re bleeding.” I looked down; indeed, narrow red rivulets flowed from my left heel. “You must have stepped on something.” Or one of Leo’s sharks took a bite out of my Achilles’ heel.

Frankly, at that point, I realized my body was shaking so violently I needed immediate warmth. Maslow’s hierarchy of needs, right? Heat first, stop the bleeding second. And who the hell cares what is third. Just give me heat. I went into the spa in search of someplace warm. Someplace, of course, was the sauna and Leo.

Leo, sans the stormtrooper regalia, welcomed us like long-lost brethren. “Come inside,” she waved us into the sauna. I dropped my robe, kicked off my flip-flops somewhere outside the entrance, and ran into the wood-paneled room. The hot sauna enveloped me, and I lay down, not caring if I offended one of the Danes by taking their seat. *Heat, warmth, I need to be thawed.* What is that saying, “Be careful what you wish for.” I closed my eyes and lost all connection with time and place as I focused on becoming human again. It was too good to last.

I heard the snap before feeling its effect. Incredibly superheated hot air cascaded on my raw, broken body. A flamethrower couldn't be worse. I bolted upright only to see Leo standing in the middle of the sauna, black gym skirt undulating from side to side, whipping a white towel through the air. Snap. More freakishly hellish air swirled around the room onto a dozen health seekers. "Arghhh," I howled.

My anguish had no impact on the Finnish devil queen. She laughed as she switched the towel from a rotary engine of death to a blanket-like torture device. Snap, she dislodged hot air from the top of the sauna and brought it down on our bodies. Snap. More flames engulfed my body and entered every pore wide open for invasion. Snap. I bent over, thinking, at least, my face would be spared. Snap. The effect of the heat was worse than the day I made the mistake of rubbing oil on my skin, thinking I rubbed on sunscreen, and then baking on a beach in Corfu one very sunny afternoon. Snap. My fellow travelers grunted as each new wave brought down thousands of needle-points on our raw, exposed skin. How much more of this shock therapy was I going to have to endure?

The snapping and waves of heat stopped, and a cool breeze signaled the fiendish vixen had departed. Another cool breeze was followed by pails of frigid water, shocking our bodies into total submission. I lay there, unable to move. Unable to think. Without any hope of this ever ending. More ice cubes melted on the wooden plank floor.

A cooing Leo returned with the wooden bucket and ladle. She dripped essential oils and water on the heated stones while chanting something in Druid or ancient Uralic. She probably had pinned a fetish doll of me to the inside of her black gym dress. Transformation again to a peaceful place. Utter collapse—I again lay down to await whatever she had in mind next. Surely the end or death must come soon.

The room again heated to its maximum, and Leo poured the rest of the bucket of water on the stones. With loud sizzles, scalding hot steam filled the room. My pores were wide open, so my skin rejected the sudden onslaught. My exposed skin burned. I jumped up—my eyes singed from the steam cloud now swirling around the ceiling of the wooden sauna chamber. I could take no more. *Escape*. I bolted from the sauna and, to my surprise, saw the entire entourage follow me out into the cool spa area. Everyone laughed, clapped each other on the back, and shook my hand. I made it out alive—salvation at last. Or so I thought.

Leo had one more trick up her sleeveless gym dress. I had never even heard of nettle tea and had no idea what it could do to me. But it sounded sharp, and I figured it would hurt. I couldn't fathom why anyone would want to put pointy things into their mouth. My group resumed talking Danish, so I took my first cup without the benefit of peer counseling. Savory, like how I imagine old wet hay tasted. I kept picturing needle-like things sliding down my gullet only to puncture my stomach. I searched in vain for sugar.

There are websites devoted to the healing properties of nettle tea. It must be an acquired taste, like raw herring. The Danes love both. And, of course, the national drink *aquavit*—which I *do* appreciate and needed now more than ever. I smiled a lot and raised my cup in cheers *en route* to find a potted plant to dispose of the tea.

I lay down on a recliner, closed my eyes, and reflected on the experience. I lived through the *saunagus*. I did feel revitalized—nothing like a dip in the cold sea to invigorate. And clearly, I had received a considerable energy kick—although, at this moment, I lay completely spent from the experience. No doubt my blood circulated at a more rapid pace than ever before—I assumed this was only temporary, and my blood pressure medicine would take effect next dose. I took it for granted that I was toxin-free—I wondered if the sauna cleaner has to wear a hazmat suit. And I'm sure my immune system hummed along at 150% as I pictured miniature nettles skewering all the bad cells in my body. I would see someone at the front desk in a few minutes about the cut on my heel—my "red badge of courage." I had survived *The Pit and the Pendulum*.

What the hell, my experience with *saunagus* would make a great short story. I got up, went over, kissed Jasmine, and then signed up to do it again the following day. Apparently, shrinkage includes the brain.

"Saunagus" was previously published in: *Lost River: A Literary Magazine*, Issue 1 (Fall 2016): 31-37.
https://issuu.com/lostriverlitmag/docs/lost_river_fall_2016_edited;
and as "Sauna Gus," *Passages: A Corrales Writing Group Anthology*, Chris Allen and Sandi Hoover, eds., North Charleston, SC: CreateSpace, January 19, 2017, pp. 61-70, and in *Anthology of Short Stories: Spring 2021*, Jilly Snowdon, ed., United Kingdom, Fenechty Publishing Anthology of Short Stories), (March 21, 2021), pp. 6-16. It was awarded Second Place in the New Mexico Press Women, New Mexico Communication 2017 Contest, Short Stories—Single Story and was the Editor's Choice in *Anthology of Short Stories: Spring 2021*.

THE ILLUSTRATED MAN

JIM TRITTEN

It had been a hard day. I downed one of those pills that would make me relax. Well, maybe two–what a day. The chairs in the Phoenix film studio had been uncomfortable. Thank goodness it's only a short evening flight to Albuquerque. I walked through the cabin closing in on seat 24B. Should be ahead on the right—an aisle seat. I can finally stretch my legs—easy access to the lavatory. Perhaps someone interesting to chat with. Someone to help me take my mind off the terrorist movie plot we worked on. Maybe that rather unusual-looking....

The first thing I noticed was his sweaty bald head as he mopped it with a white paper napkin. He looked up, and we made eye contact. I smiled politely. In return, his wide grin revealed a gold front tooth. He turned back to his submarine sandwich, stuffing the remainder into his mouth while crumbs and condiments rained down on his lap.

I swung into 24B, adjacent to his window seat, and was welcomed by the smell of grilled onions. I glanced to my left. Grease drooled from his lips, down his chin, and onto his black T-shirt. *Just my luck, there's no seat between us.* The white napkin returned to his pate, and he again wiped sweat. Perspiration saturated the paper.

I craned my neck searching for an empty seat. *Perhaps there's a couple who wants to sit together. I'd trade seats. No, that won't work; only two seats on this side of the plane. Maybe there's a couple who doesn't want to sit together.*

The flight attendant confirmed my fears. "This flight is completely full. Please place your carry-on luggage in the bin overhead or under the seat in front of you."

When she said a full flight, does that include first class? I've got enough miles for an upgrade.

"The captain has closed the door. Please fasten your seat belts and turn off all electronic devices."

I pretended to look past my neighbor out the window at the ground crew as the plane rolled backward. He was probably in his early thirties —no facial hair like I have.

Oh! Tattoos. How did I miss these?

They ran up from under his T-shirt onto his neck, reaching up to the base of his skull—reminded me of wisteria climbing the base of a giant oak. More crept down from his short sleeves, practically obliterating any unmarked skin. Mostly blue ink with a smattering of red intertwining the designs and words. His powerful, greasy fingers sported a variety of polished steel rings. One featured a skull and crossbones.

"Good evening, this is your captain. The flight to Albuquerque will take forty-five minutes. We expect clear skies and no turbulence."

Really? Not from where I sit. I reached up and turned on the air conditioning, shifting the flow to the left ever so slightly. I tightened my seatbelt and clenched my jaw.

~

"Whatasuv he saoidnag hwu lungae to Alvaquanaiue?"

My travel companion creased his brow, suggesting that whatever he said was a question. *What did he say?* The man was obviously mumbling. I looked to my left, and again we made eye contact. Grease continued to drip down from his lips.

"Whatasuv he saoidnag hwu lungae to Alvaquanaiue?" he repeated while airborne saliva, caramelized onions, and meat flecks flew at me. Probably a Philly cheesesteak.

This time I caught a glimpse of studs in his tongue as he attempted to verbalize what I surmised were words in English. *What's he asking me?* I ventured a guess.

"I think the captain said we would be airborne for about forty-five minutes. With taxi time, we should be at the gate in an hour."

"Thasnilk." His head nodded up and down. He smiled, and the gold in his mouth shone. Then he coughed into the formerly white napkin, depositing green chunks of what were probably either chiles or jalapenos.

No wonder he couldn't speak straight. Too hot for you, heh?

The engines roared, and we rolled forward on the runway. Out of the corner of my eye, I saw the nasty napkin get scrunched up and put inside the greasy waxed paper from his sandwich. He stuffed the mess into the magazine pouch at his knees and wiped his hands on his shirt —first the palms. Then the backs and then each finger. His biceps and forearm muscles were well-developed. Each flexed, animating his illustrated skin. *Wonder what they'll look like when he's seventy?*

I closed my eyes and stroked my beard and mustache as we lifted off into the moonlit skies.

After reaching cruising altitude and being alerted it was safe, I unbuckled my seatbelt and bent forward to reach under the seat in front. My backpack containing my iPad was wedged firmly underneath. His leg leaned into my space and blocked my backpack. As my head twisted to the left, the chrome studs of the man's leather trousers reflected the overhead reading lights. His trouser legs were tucked into high black leather boots. A slack, polished chain ran down the side of the trousers, affixed by a bolt screwed into the heel of his boot.

"Excuse me, sir. Would you please move your leg so I can get my backpack?"

"Oh coirhsaj," he muttered as the offending limb retracted into his domain.

I reached down and pulled out the backpack. As I withdrew my iPad and put it on my lap, the man took out a large smartphone. He held it close to his face. *Wonder what he's looking at?* If I pushed my head back into my seat, I could detect he was playing some kind of game. It had his attention. His thumbs continued to press buttons, eliciting an occasional animalistic grunt or groan from the player. The red wallpaper on his phone had a black circle in the center. Inside this circle, there was a white design——blocked from view by the game. My eyes widened as I realized the tips of the design in four distinct corners were clearly the edges of a swastika inside the black circle.

All thoughts of using my iPad were replaced by searching my memory for what I knew about the Aryan Brotherhood. *The Brotherhood used swastika tattoos. They grew out of prisons—have they moved into New Mexico? Which tattoo is awarded after the initiate kills his first victim? What if I told him I used to own a Harley?*

Maybe he's a Hells Angel? Too bad I couldn't read the lettering on the T-shirt. I used to wear leather trousers when I owned a Harley. I never wore a helmet and often rode with a cop back in D.C. Hadn't thought about that cop for years. He had been shot while trying to arrest a killer.

The illustrated man is a paid killer. Yeah, that's it. A hitman hired by the patrónes, the Hispanic bosses, coming into Albuquerque to do a job. Probably drug-related. So how will he get a weapon to do the job? Did he check it with his luggage, or would he pick up a clean piece in New Mexico? Not like it's hard to get a weapon in our state. He would have some new type of weapon they write about in all those thrillers—a Glock. I think most of them use Glocks. Or an Uzi.

The flight attendant broke my thoughts. "Sir, would you like to have a beverage?"

"Yes, give me a rum and coke. No, make it two." *What I really need are more pills.*

"Ikansgpu anseu cocknue?" The man eyed my soft drink as it was handed to me.

The flight attendant looked puzzled and then smiled as she replied, "The attendant up front has the coffee. I'll get you some in a minute."

"No, *Ikansgpu anseu cocknue?"*

I sensed the illustrated man wanted a Coke like mine and suggested, "I think he'd like a Coke."

Good guess. I wouldn't want hot coffee if my tongue had been burned already by that sandwich. The illustrated man grunted, and I was rewarded again with another look at his gold tooth. The attendant served him a Diet Coke, and I kept my mouth shut when he accepted it without comment.

I mixed my drink and emptied the plastic cup. I leaned back and closed my eyes. *Okay, calm yourself.* The alcohol felt good as the cool liquid went down my throat and into my churning belly. The second tasted better but not enough to quench my unsettled mind. Before I knew it, I was off to the races again—monkey brain bouncing ideas off the inside of my cranium.

I knew we all went through the TSA security check. *He doesn't have a weapon on him right now. But why would the agents allow an obvious killer like this to get on the plane? Don't we have the right to sit in safety?*

Don't the counter agents have some kind of profile this guy should have met? Why did they give him a boarding pass? See if I ever fly this airline again.

Is there an air marshal on this plane? Yeah, he can deal with this guy. I don't have to. Not my job. God, is this plane hot.

The man clicked away at his game. *How many kills was he getting? Was he whacking them or shooting at them like in the old Atari Space Invaders? Maybe the game was a ruse, and what he's actually doing is planning a mass murder in Old Town. That's it; the white supremacists are going to make a statement about the takeover of America by Hispanics. No, wait, the Spanish were here first in New Mexico. Is this guy the mysterious highway assassin who was shooting drivers on the Phoenix interstates last week? I need to warn them.*

I unbuckled my seatbelt and was about to get up and talk to the cabin attendant, but I was interrupted.

"Wharoaiun asnuagub kounuean?"

Again, his eyebrows rose. I guessed it was a question.

I put my finger in my ear, raised an eyebrow, and frowned.

"Wharoaiun asnuagub kounuean?"

Better not offend this killer. What does he want? I offered an answer. "We should be on the ground in about a half-hour." He grunted and went back to planning mass murder.

Or is he planning my murder? He probably knows a dozen ways to kill me in my seat. He could put a knife between my ribs and deflate one of my lungs. I saw a show on the television where the victim never even felt the blade. No, he can't have a knife on the plane. But if he takes one of his thick arms and reaches around my back, he could snap my spine. Stop it.

I leaned forward and felt behind me. The man looked at me. I put my iPad back into my backpack, then put the backpack under the seat in front of me.

So, if this guy is, in fact, a hired killer, does he know that I know? Will he need to silence me before he gets off the plane? He will have to make it seem like an accident.

I moved as far over to the right in my seat as I could and closed my eyes. The drinks and the pills began to work, and I was enveloped in total silence, blackness, and the faint smell of caramelized onions.

The bump of the landing brought me back to consciousness as the plane touched down. I felt along the left side of my torso for any sticky wet spots—my fingertips were dry. *So far, so good.* I pulled out my backpack. The plane taxied into the ramp area. *Jesus, why is this taking so long?* After it stopped, I got out of my seat and stood patiently in the aisle—my eyes rigidly fixed ahead.

The other passengers hurried from the plane. I rudely pushed ahead of anyone I could and bolted down the aisle to safety. The aircraft deck shook as the heavy boots behind me thudded in cadence with the light touch of my Birkenstocks. *Why didn't I wear closed shoes? Is he going to follow me outside to the parking lot?* I raced down the terminal corridors, aware of the internal pressure directing me to find the nearest toilet. *Is it safe?*

I lost the sound of boots as I whisked through the turnstile, passing close by the TSA agent monitoring the portal. *It should be safe now.* I stopped and turned around. Nothing. The illustrated man wasn't anywhere in sight. I let out a long sigh and wondered how the agent could have helped. *Don't they know there are people in mortal danger here?* I ran into the bathroom.

Stay in the bathroom until everyone claims their luggage and leaves the terminal. That was the plan. *Might as well be safe than sorry.*

After what seemed an eternity, I emerged from the bathroom. Directly in front of me, my eyes spied the familiar black T-shirt and leather trousers of the illustrated man walking toward the escalator. The polished chain swung loosely at the side of his leg. A glint of light reflected from his gold tooth. *He's still here.*

I slid into an alcove, steeling myself for defense should he turn and spot me. I peered around a potted plant. The man held hands with a beautiful, tall woman about his age. She was slim and wore flowers in her long wavy blonde hair, which flowed freely as she chattered. She wore a pale blue and white dress that danced to the rhythm of her step.

Alongside the woman, five young giggling children skipped, carrying toy bears in their arms. They bobbed for attention alongside the couple as they moved toward the escalator.

One of the little children pointed at me, grimaced, and cried. The tall blonde woman glanced at me, picked up the child, and as they continued forward, I heard her say, "He's probably a nice man. We shouldn't be so quick to judge."

Earlier and slightly different versions of this story appeared as: "21st Century Illustrated Man" *Caesura Journal*, Issue 3 (December 8, 2016): 35-42; "21st Century Illustrated Man," *Passages: A Corrales Writing Group Anthology*, Chris Allen and Sandi Hoover, eds., North Charleston, SC: CreateSpace, January 19, 2017, pp. 5-12; "The

Illustrated Man," *As You Were: The Military Review*, May 29, 2017, http://militaryexperience.org/the-illustrated-man/, and in *Stories Through The Ages Baby Boomers Plus 2020*, Centennial, CO, Living Springs Publishers, October 3, 2020, pp. 224-244. An earlier, shorter (1026 word) version was awarded the Gold Medal for 1st Place at the 2016 National Veterans Creative Arts Festival in Jackson, Mississippi, in October 2016.

GUARDIAN CACTUS

SANDI HOOVER

Jo gasped and squinted. The sun singed her entire body after stepping outside Tucson International's icy air conditioning. Slamming on dark glasses, she reread the text saying Sammie was on her way. She inhaled and her shoulders slowly dropped as she stood at the curb, soaking up the colors and flavor of the landscape.

"Is it the quality of light, the freedom of space, maybe the aromas, no, it's the warmth—actually heat—no, something else, but it feels like an old friend welcoming me back…want this," Jo mumbled softly to herself as she basked in the sunshine. She understood why the lizard on the nearby prickly pear was stretched out with its eyes closed. *You look content. Full tummy and a safe place to sleep. I'll like that too.* She sent good thoughts to the dozing reptile.

"Hey Jocelyn…Jo, wake up!" Sammie shouted through the open window on the passenger side of the dust-covered car. "Throw your suitcase in the back, and hop in so I don't keep blocking traffic."

Snapping out of her daydream, Jo did as she was told and climbed onto the old 4Runner's battered seat, leaned to proffer a quick, almost-hug and air-kiss to her dearest friend, and buckled up.

"Yahoo! You're finally here! I wasn't sure you were going to allow yourself to have some fun. You've been such a workaholic, even canceling our last vacation time. I can't wait to show you my town and give you a spicy taste of the old Southwest."

Jo leaned back and smiled. "I am ready for anything you have to offer, girlfriend. I feel like this is home, and you may be stuck with me longer than you think. I can't believe it's taken so many years for me to visit here. Where's the first margarita?"

"Just about fifteen minutes away," Sammie replied with a huge grin. "Lean back, relax and leave the driving to us. That tagline still works. We'll catch up over a good cold drink that will make you forget old what's his name."

"That can't happen soon enough. What started as a healthy relationship became abusive and frightening before I could break free. Ted's violent behavior and heavy drinking is one reason I want distance between us. He was also the reason I canceled our trip last year. He made it very clear I was not to leave him."

"Jeez Jo, I had no idea. You camouflaged your situation well."

"Being constantly watched and listened to made it hard to be honest, and I thought I could make everything right if I worked at it. I knew better. Some psychologist I am. I told others not to anticipate changing someone, but it didn't apply to me. Silly me. Well, enough of that. Lead me to a margarita."

A few more blocks and Sammie parked in front of a Bougainvillea-covered structure whose arches defined a cool patio with a tiered fountain's peaceful sounds adding to the atmosphere.

A margarita and an order of guacamole prefaced a lengthy meal and another margarita, while Sammie encouraged Jo to share her experience dealing with emotional and finally, physical violence in the abusive situation she had fled.

"I didn't tell anyone what I was enduring. I guess, even though I knew better intellectually, I thought somehow I was to blame. Your invitation was the galvanizing thing I needed to break loose and escape. Thanks for not writing me off after I bailed out last year."

"Jo, you may be an idiot for staying with Ted after the first incident, but you're my friend and important to me. So let's banish Ted. We'll smother him with honey. You haven't met our version of *beignets*. *Sopaipillas* are one of the best desserts, at least three food groups since they are honey-filled, fried, puffy pastry. You bite off one corner and soak the interior with honey. This place makes the best! When we're stuffed, we'll see what the rest of today brings."

Sammie gave Jo a tour of Tucson's old town and the museum area, then headed for the Sonora Desert Museum and a look at the native plants and the views of the mountains surrounding the city. The afternoon of being shown the highlights, and Jo's own further examination in the following days, reinforced her first impression.

"I love everything about Tucson. I'm staying! I'll make new memories here and rediscover myself," she told Sammie several days later.

Not long after, she called Sammie, rejoicing. "Would you believe I've found a perfect place for my home and office. The price is right because it's an iffy neighborhood now, but the area is changing, the view is unbelievable, and I'll make sure I'm safe. I'll call you when I'm back from Vermont. Wahoo!"

Back east, she faced a swift round of closing her counseling business, selling things, packing and shipping, and then driving cross country. Reaching Tucson, Jo disappeared into her new life, organizing her business, getting certified, and completing insurance applications, indicating her availability to counsel clients dealing with substance abuse and addiction. She painted walls and brought her favorite things out of boxes. After settling in, she made a trip to a local nursery and spent hours wandering among desert flora until she was drawn to a pair of Silver Torch cactus plants. These were over five feet tall and gracefully fluted with shiny silver fuzz, decorating myriad spines. She had them potted and delivered to her second-floor loft.

After they were placed on her balcony, Jo carefully unwrapped the protective paper and plastic covering.

"You are even more dramatic than I thought at the nursery. Backlit right now, you look delicate and furry, but I know… yipes," she sucked a finger, stuck as she was carelessly waving a hand. "Well, that proved how sharp your covering of spines is. After your upheaval, you need time to adjust to me and this place."

Next morning, Jo carried a bucket of water to her balcony and set it on the tiny table designated for daybreak coffee. Breathing deeply, she took a minute to revel yet again in the view of mountains beyond the piles of used wood and metal in the fenced lot in the foreground and then turned to the cactus near her and spoke slowly and softly to it.

"You are now one of my two special guardians. You, *Narasimha,* the man-lion, are not only beautiful, you are fierce and majestic, and I know you, along with your brother, will keep me and my home safe from intruders." Standing motionless, she tingled with the conviction she was being examined and considered. Jo inhaled, consciously noting her sense of connection to the earth and the plant in front of her, noticing cinnamon spice and warm desert dust in air still chilly from the previous night.

She poured half the water into *Narasimha's* pot before she took the few steps to the other end of the balcony. Jo soberly repeated the same mantra to the remaining cactus. "You are beautiful and majestic and have the power to keep me safe. You, *Parashurama*, my warrior-priest, are also a special guardian. I am grateful to have you and your brother standing watch over me." Again she felt a connection to the silvery plant whose columns ended at her eye level.

Jo's relaxed posture reflected her mood as she stood on her balcony, reliving that happy day over a year ago. She closed her eyes and lifted her face to the sun, warming her as it peeped over the mountain beyond the industrial wasteland in the foreground. "Mmmm, that's scrumptious," she said, first hugging herself, stretching on tiptoes, then spreading her arms wide to welcome the day although the chill had her bundled in a heavy sweater.

"Alright, boys, here we are, facing another beautiful day," she said to *Narasimha* and *Parashurama.* Soak up this sun and fresh air before you are brought in tonight since there is a freeze predicted." She poured some water from a pitcher into each pot as she spoke to them as if they were sentient beings.

"It's a good thing you two are set on casters. Otherwise, even with help I couldn't move you! You've grown tremendously, and your deep red blooms were glorious. Now that they're spent, I'll get my gloves and remove them before you come in so they don't fall inside. You'll enjoy the grooming." With one last smile and blown kisses to each of them, she closed the sliding glass door and prepared to see her first client.

Several clients later she left her combo home and office to meet Sammie at La Parilla Suiza for lunch.

Sammie's words tumbled out in a rush as she found Jo already seated. "Hey, Jo! I thought I would see more of you when we lived in the same city. Are you pleased with the increasing number of clients and work? Are the cacti still happy on the balcony? It's been nearly four months since we had our last margarita together, so let's order one and lunch and talk."

"I'm ready," Jo answered. "No clients this afternoon so I'm delighted to linger over *sopaipillas*, and make lunch a total splurge. The business is growing, and the last fourteen months have been overwhelmingly busy, but totally satisfying. I think now I can set a different schedule with more free time."

They talked non-stop while sipping lime-flavored drinks. Fish tacos and guacamole hardly interrupted their conversation as they exchanged news and the small talk of good friendship.

More months sped by, holidays passed, time was made for hiking and parties, and in Jo's counseling room clients came and went, as both cactuses stood silently, holding their spine-filled trunks at attention.

Writing client notes while sipping a mid-afternoon mug of tea, Jo sat at her tiny table, tucked into a corner of the office room for the winter season. Watching a band of sunshine move across the opposite wall, she stopped writing and happily remembered the start of her new life. *What a whirlwind of change. Splendiferous, magical change. No idea transformation could happen in a heartbeat. Just the first glimpse of a Mesquite tree's lacy foliage, and the solid, old Spanish-influenced architecture, with palm trees and cactus everywhere, and the Saguaros...how could I have lived so long where there were no Saguaros?*

"I love it all, and you two guardians are an important part of it." She looked left and right and nodded to her two, very tall, very spiny, multi-limbed cactus plants, waiting patiently for their return to her small balcony.

A few minutes later as she finished her write-ups, there was a knock, the door burst open and a large, disheveled man strode in, early for his appointment.

"I f-ing don't believe it!" The angry bass voice of Mack, Jo's newest client, filled her office. "My old lady just left me! No warning, not telling me she was unhappy! She just bugged out while I was at work!" The anger in his voice grew louder and overrode his sorrow, as his ire and frustration found an outlet. Jo leapt to her feet without thinking and took two steps back, putting her up against the wall behind her.

Red faced, he sputtered swear words in a loud stream, not allowing Jo to interject a comment. He threw himself into the comfortable chair placed for clients, still screaming. "Not only that, she stole my computer, and the new microwave too! All she left was a 'fuck you' note."

Jo gasped in spite of trying for calm. *No, no, this is not happening*. She was flashing back to her terror of her live-in boyfriend in Vermont. His alcoholic rages sounded too much like Mack's violent words.

"Mack," she started, but was interrupted as he screamed more obscenities, then continued without a pause. "That miserable bitch, if I see her again, I'll teach her not to mess with me! She can't use me for a bed and meals and steal..." He shook his raised fist as if to punch someone in the face.

Jo took a breath as he continued his rant, concentrating on finding the right words, working to achieve a balance. A slight motion caused her to look up in time to see *Narasimha* toppling slowly toward Mack. She blanched, her mouth frozen open in shock, as the cactus gained speed in its inexorable fall.

"THE PERFECT WOMAN"

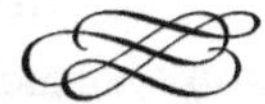

JIM TRITTEN

"...And, therefore, she is the perfect woman."

I confess, my mind was sort of wandering—until I heard our friend Brit say "...and therefore, she is the perfect woman." My wife of then twenty-five years Jasmine and I were visiting a small rural farm in western Sweden. We gazed at an idyllic green pasture with a burnt-red-colored barn standing atop a slight rise. The wind washed over us from our backs—smells from the barnyard remained downwind. Orange, yellow, and blue flowers adorned boxes on a rustic two-story white and blue cottage. It was a brisk, overcast day in May. Piles of dirty snow littered the outlying tree line. Summer was still an unfulfilled promise. Horses, cows, sheep, goats, ducks, chickens, and other animals ran amok but kept their distance from us, the trespassers. Obviously, they did not trust city folk. Beautiful setting...but I digress.

"Brit, what did you just say?"

"My friend raises her own food, has her own animals, and when it comes time, she slaughters her own sheep. She takes them around the side of her house, so when she kills them, the other animals do not see. She is the perfect woman."

Brit recounted this with a straight face, clearly confused why I did not understand what she said. English was *not* her native language, but I did comprehend her words. Jasmine and I have known Brit for over twenty-five years… she introduced us. Today, she had taken us across the border from her native Norway to a friend's farm in Sweden, where she was now extolling that person's virtues.

I closed my mouth and pondered. Was this female Swedish farmer, capable of slaughtering her own sheep, "The Perfect Woman?" Was she the perfect woman because she was a self-sufficient agriculturalist? Or was the critical element killing her own sheep? I asked for clarification. Was sheep homicide the vital criterion? The answer was yes; Brit confirmed to us it was mammalian ruminant slaughter that made her friend the perfect woman. Jasmine and I glanced at each other; she knew I was hooked on a quest.

Who is "The Perfect Woman?" What are her attributes?

I took a photograph of the property with sheep grazing placidly on the newly-grown grasses, oblivious of their impending doom. I posted the photo on Facebook and noted this place as the home of "The Perfect Woman." I added my intent to do some research and then write an essay on the subject of "The Perfect Woman" when we finished our trip to Scandinavia.

I also "friended" one of the Norwegian men we met on the other side of the border. Within a minute, my new friend Bjørn "liked" my posting about the Swedish farm and finding the location of "The Perfect Woman." Brit told us Bjørn had a history with this mysterious female farmer, now known as "The Perfect Woman." Not wanting to upset delicate Norwegian-Swedish relations, I did not ask any intrusive questions.

Upon our return to the U.S., I told a few people about my latest quest for knowledge and received lots of advice. I was warned not to cross some lines that could get me into trouble. Hence, the need for disclaimers. Let me make it quite clear. In my search for "The Perfect Woman," I disqualify all wives, grandmothers, mothers, daughters, sisters, aunts, nieces, or anyone's other relatives. After all, most of these women are reminded with a Hallmark product, flowers, and candy annually they are, in fact, "perfect." These specific women should and will remain sacrosanct and out of bounds for my intended tongue-in-cheek investigation.

Having now stepped into the minefield and perhaps defused a few of the more obvious Claymores, I need to deal with perspective. I recently attended the San Miguel de Allende International Writers' Conference in Mexico, where I listened for hours while some well-known feminists expounded familiar themes to wildly enthusiastic audiences. To make their point for them, I am fully aware each woman should be the sole judge of her value or "perfectness." What some man thinks should not be the basis for any woman's self-worth. I do not dispute this view.

That acknowledged, there seems to be a universe of differing opinions on what constitutes value, worth, or what constitutes "The Perfect Woman." Indicators from these ill-informed parts of society "may," and according to the feminist speakers in Mexico, often "do" conflict with what those speakers told us "should be" in a "perfect" world. My essay is not about what the perfect woman "ought" to be, but rather what society tells women is the answer.

Let's try lobbing this hand grenade out and see if I survive the frag pattern.

Is the perfect woman defined primarily by physical characteristics?

Women of striking physical beauty are regularly featured by photographers in popular magazines, as news anchors and weather reporters, and as models for high fashion. These women are judged by others as being attractive and then featured in the public media. The criterion often is magnificence as quickly assessed by the naked eye… not the more complex standards for inner beauty.

A cursory review of the subject of "The Perfect Woman" on the Internet leads anyone into the area of physical beauty, with websites tracing the silhouette of women through the ages. The shapes have varied over time, with one of the current aspects of measurement being thigh gap. It seems most of these sites are very Eurocentric. I saw few women of color and never saw images of the women in Africa with neck rings I recall from my childhood readings of *National Geographic*. None of the women featured at the time appeared with sheep or the means of dispatching them at the end of their lives.

Where else to look? When you Google "The Perfect Woman," you can find opinion polls on what many people think is the perfect woman. For example, some 100,000 men who use the *What's Your Price* dating service voiced their opinion on what constituted the ideal woman. Their answer was someone with blonde hair, blue eyes, a slender body, a non-smoker, and a social drinker who has earned a graduate degree. At least they threw a bone at a woman's mind. We should note these opinions are taken from a database where the survey participants *buy* their first dates.

The rebuttal to this obviously flawed view of perfection was voiced by Ellen DeGeneres. Her view of what men should want in a perfect woman is someone who will challenge you intellectually, someone who is empathetic, accepts you for YOU—no mention of any physical traits here. Perhaps there is a difference between what men say they want and what women say men *should* want? Why did neither the men seeking dates nor Ellen mention sheep?

Additional surveys over the years have asked men what it is they are looking for in a woman. While we can't know for certain, we can assume respondents would be describing their ideal when filling out the survey instruments. In general, Ellen should be pleased there seems to be more of a balance between beauty and brains in other assessments.

For example, *Men's Health* magazine, in its December 9, 2012 issue, reported of the eleven qualities of the perfect woman, more than a third were defined by *other than* physical aspects. The article, written by a woman, references various serious reports and studies and concludes there are qualities found in women that men find attractive. These criteria include ladies who laugh at a man's jokes, a female who smiles, someone who can pull her own weight, and a woman with an education.

I admit one of the most attractive features I initially noticed in Jasmine was her captivating smile. One of the qualities I did not appreciate until I started writing for fun was her laughing at my humorous articles.

Returning to the main point, the author tells *Men's Health* readers specifically what men want in a woman's career:

"**Careers Are Sexy** Are the days of the trophy wife over? Science seems to think so. According to a study published in the *American Journal of Sociology*, when men were asked about the makeup of their ideal partner, a majority claimed they're looking for a woman who can economically pull her own weight in the relationship. See ya later, gold diggers."

Regarding education, the author of this article states:

"**Intelligence Is Refreshing** The days of the dumb blonde are done, too. According to research published in *The Journal of Sex Research*, men reported being more satisfied when their partner had an adequate educational background. But at the same time, men also reported less marital satisfaction when the female was the breadwinner of the family. So success is hot—just not too much success."

There are other indicators of what society views as perfection in women. For example, many groups organize contests reflecting something about the embodiment of women in their countries, states, counties, municipalities, etc. None of these "meat markets" define the winners as "perfect," but the implication is they could be described as approaching one possible paradigm of perfection. Most of these contests assess women wearing formal wear, a swimsuit, and the results of a personality interview. Talent is ignored in many of these contests except perhaps rodeo queens and pie bakes. I wonder if there is any contest in which the compassion in killing sheep is measured with numbered cards. For the record, the Miss Universe New Zealand application mentions nothing about sheep (yes, I checked).

Many men think they found the perfect woman and enter into a living arrangement, or marriage, leading to the production of offspring. Some later discover their initial assessment was wrong. A young couple marrying for the first time today has a lifetime divorce risk of around 40 percent. But millions of individuals think their partner is at least perfect enough to marry and/or have their children. Where *are* they getting their advice? From their hearts or other parts of their bodies and not what Ellen tells us men we should want?

Let's toss another hand grenade—the Barbie Doll. Barbie launched in March 1959. The original doll was accused of and, in fact, presented an unrealistic body image to young women. Young boys I knew thought Barbie was hot. The fear was girls who attempted to emulate Barbie would develop eating disorders. I thought Barbie had been run out of town by now. I did not see any Barbie Dolls for sale at the San Miguel de Allende Writers' Conference. I did notice, however, photographs of Gloria Steinem in her Playboy Bunny outfit.

Mattel markets these dolls today with optional physical appearances and numerous accessories to highlight some two hundred careers and lifestyle choices open to women. Today's themes include empowering women, inspiring women, "you can be anything," and role models emphasizing diversity. Check out their website and make up your own mind.

Now for some related anecdotal evidence. I've dated one of two identical twins—more than once in my life. One pair was similar to the Barbie Doll model. Drop-dead gorgeous. One might describe them as physically perfect—both of them. One laughed at my jokes, always smiled because she always seemed to see the good side of anything.

She had what had previously been considered a man's job where she made good money and had a college degree with aspirations of further education. She could drink most men under the table and played a mean hand of liar's dice at the bar. She was also immensely helpful to me at a time I needed assistance.

Unfortunately, she was married to a really good guy and pulled her own weight in the relationship. He was a Navy SEAL. I never dated this one or the SEAL. However, her identical twin sister came to town one weekend, and I needed to repay my benefactor a big favor. So, I agreed to take out the twin…

…how could I go wrong?

I learned the sister spent her days working out at the gym and watching television. That's it. I can recall no other activities. She had an exercise bike in front of her TV. Conversation was strained at best. I believe that the words "have you ever read a book" slipped out of my mouth while I was attempting to make small talk on my one and only date. So much for beauty alone being the sole criterion for perfection. At least for me.

The arts are often accused of leading society, but, more often, they reflect society. We should be able to learn something about what artists consider the perfect woman by looking at paintings, music, films, literature, etc.

One of the more oft-recognized views is women as depicted in paintings. The artist Peter Paul Rubens had a distinct view of the perfect woman. His fondness of painting full-figured women gave rise to the terms' Rubensian' or 'Rubenesque' for so-called 'plus-sized' women. The settings for Ruben's women rarely gave a hint of their occupation. They often appeared in the nude alongside men whose professions might be surmised by what they wore. Artists often capture women on canvas without any apparent reference to a work. In the multitude of websites that trace the ideal woman over the ages, there are ample changes in clothing. The examples of attire for these women are all social and rarely provide a hint at any professions…other than Little Bo Peep.

Most nations have a symbol of national personification used for everything from military recruiting posters to postage stamps and on currency. In France, this is Marianne; in Greece, it is Athena; and in the Netherlands, it is the Dutch Maiden. In the United States, it is Columbia. These national icons are physically appealing, although not necessarily attractive. The French are always different. Since 1969, Marianne has undergone modifications to resemble living famous and beautiful people. The two most well-known are Bridget Bardot and Catherine Deneuve.

Some recording artists have used the phrase "perfect woman" in songs. Bo Burnham describes one of his perfect women as blind and another as someone who didn't talk too much. Pat Dailey and Macaw tell us their ideal woman is a rich, dumb, young nymphomaniac who owns a liquor store. Several songwriters manage to fit in something about a liquor store when describing the perfect woman—even more than referring to them as blondes. Adrian Belew wrote a song called "The Ideal Woman." This person is described as demure, friendly, a loving person, religious, great personality, fun to be with, fashionable, romantic, talented, creative, wealthy, independent, powerful, liberal, controllable, silent, good-looking, tall, thin, blonde, sexy, pretty with hairy legs. Belew adds she is my wife and my mother.

It's a long song.

There are around nine films with the title "The Perfect Woman." The earliest appeared in 1920. This movie is listed as a romantic comedy, but not much else is known about the film. It starred Constance Talmage, who we can assume was film's first "perfect woman." Her biography lists her as blonde, buoyant, and a comedienne.

The next film to use the title "The Perfect Woman" did not appear until 1949. The film stars two different actresses. One plays a robot. The film documents man's attempt to *create* a perfect woman. The second actress performs as the human model for the robot. The male lead chooses the human over the android in the end. Once again, art shows us mankind can't improve upon nature. We cannot create a perfect woman. Creating perfect creatures didn't work with the Frankenstein monster or his bride. But this story keeps getting told—implying what? The biography for the actress playing the human model lists her as being pretty, vivacious, and charming.

A 1993 comedic short, "The Perfect Woman," features a series of unnamed women talking to men during attempted pickups. This film is written, directed, and produced by a female member of the cast. The storyline for this film in the Internet Movie Database (IMDb) website says:

"The women, who are desperate for affection and a relationship, apologize, bend over backwards to accommodate, cooperate with every male fantasy, tolerate every male insecurity, ignore infidelities, and pick up the check."

If you thought Hollywood was going to provide an in-depth answer to who is the perfect woman, I guess you believe film versions of a story are better than books. My money is generally on the book being more complex and satisfying (*The Thin Man* being a notable exception). So, let's see what the world of traditional publication offers.

The words "perfect woman" or "women" have been used in scores of books, short stories, and even on the funny pages of newspapers. The bulk of these are self-help books for individuals in search of or wanting to advertise themselves as the perfect woman. A few of these books cross the line into illustrated erotica (sorry, no citations—find them yourself). There are also a fair number of romances using the title. Some are mysteries in which the women slain are generally considered by the killer as not being perfect. Of note are sci-fi offerings paralleling themes found in Hollywood where man tries to create an ideal woman, such as in *Metropolis* or *The Bride of Frankenstein*. In one of these sci-fi books, the author's premise is that man cannot compete with the innate power of women (I know I have felt this way upon occasion). The author claims only through science will man be able to find what he needs. In J.D. Reed's April 2015 story "He's the Perfect Woman," a man eats a magical cookie that transforms him into a beautiful female with an uncontrolled sex drive.

In addition to the two bad witches, the 1900 book *The Wonderful Wizard of Oz* by Lyman Frank Baum features two good witches. The Wicked Witch of the East dies with the arrival of Dorothy in Munchkinland. Baum makes it clear this sorceress had wreaked havoc on the Munchkins and deserved to die. Baum depicts the surviving Wicked Witch of the West as bitter, full of rage, yet powerful. Margaret Hamilton, aided by Jack Young's superb but hideous makeup, wonderfully portrays the Wicked Witch of the West in the 1939 movie *The Wizard of Oz*. Message to the audience, negative characteristics and bad looks accompany characters who are evil and cause problems.

In the book, there are two separate good witches. The Good Witch of the North initially meets Dorothy in Munchkinland. She is elderly, her face covered with wrinkles, her hair nearly white, and she walks rather stiffly. Although she is kind, she is not powerful enough to help the young girl immediately return to Kansas. She does provide a protective kiss on Dorothy's forehead, safeguarding her journey into the Land of Oz.

In the movie, there is only one good witch with a speaking role, Glinda, the Good Witch of the South. Billie Burke expertly portrayed Glinda in the film. Rather than with Good Witch of the North, she appears in Munchkinland to provide the initial guidance to Dorothy. Her attributes? Glinda is young, beautiful, dressed as a princess, wise, merciful, and helps Dorothy's traveling companions get what they want. In both the book and movie, Glinda helps Dorothy return to Kansas at the end of the story. She also frees the Winged Monkeys. Get the differences? Can we agree on what would be attributes of the perfect woman here? Do these images of "perfection" provided to children last a lifetime?

Cartoons in America often also mirror society. In 1950, Al Capp took his character Li'l Abner on a year-long journey searching for the perfect woman. Li'l Abner finds a torn photo showing a mystery woman's knee. He falls in love with just the physical beauty of the knee, and the search commences. His quest takes him to outer space, to a mythical hot country filled with beautiful women and sleepy men, to the corridors of political power and, of all places, Brooklyn.

Given the intellectual depth of cartoons, it is unlikely the criteria for perfection went beyond the physical.

If we turn to poetry, perhaps we can escape from the visual depictions of perfection and address flawlessness from a more refined perspective. Poets can capture the essence of an issue in fewer words than I. There are many poems about the perfect woman. I will refer to two.

William Wordsworth, author of "I Wandered Lonely as a Cloud," wrote about his wife in a poem known either as "The Perfect Woman" or "The Phantom of Delight." The first two parts of the entire work depict when the couple first met. In these initial sections, Wordsworth recognizes and acknowledges her beauty. In the second section, as they get to know each other, he admits she works hard to please him as his wife. Only in the final segment the author recognizes her spirit of happiness and tries to capture what makes her the perfect woman. Wordsworth mentions attributes such as a firm reason, a temperate will, endurance, foresight, strength, skill, able to warn, comfort, and command, a spirit still and bright, with something of an "angelic light."

A more contemporary poem with the title "The Perfect Woman" is written from the perspective of a female, Sylvia Chidi. Attributes include standing elegantly tall, staring right at you, displaying motherly kindness, exhibiting contemporary greatness, charm, with a disarming smile, serving as a positive role model and able to affect the lives of others, an outstanding personality, intellect, plain and straightforward, without flaws, and always following the law. The repeated refrain—the perfect woman is the woman all girls want to be.

A few authors and famous men in life are quoted in simple prose consisting of just a few lines of pure opinion. My favorite is the view of that well-known international rabble-rouser, social scientist, political theorist, philosopher, father of Marxist theory, and author of *The Communist Manifesto*, Friedrich Engels. According to the Goodreads website of great quotations, Freddy said:

"If there were no Frenchwomen, life wouldn't be worth living."

I wonder whether he shared this view with Karl Marx? Moreover, what do Frenchwomen have to do with the withering away of the state? Engels was ahead of his time—he did not live to witness Marianne being modeled after a young Bridget Bardot or Catherine Deneuve.

In modern times, views on any subject can be found in the digital universe. There are many perfect women hits on Facebook, but by far, the most revealing were found on Twitter. Some women advertise themselves to be "perfect." The most direct appeal comes from someone who said:

"I'll make you a sandwich and fetch you a beer, then talk sports over dinner."

That particular tweet was subsequently deleted before I could find a non-attached male friend to do follow-up research. So, I decided to take a non-scientific survey on Facebook and asked my "friends" if they had any opinions on what constituted the perfect woman. Here are a smattering of replies—written mainly by women:

"I think the perfect woman would be neurotic…on the inside because everyone (on the outside) thinks she's perfect. Maybe she isn't even real, maybe an excellent hologram, robotic or non-human. Personally, I'd find a "perfect" person to be irritating. Hate being around someone who's always right."

"Someone who can stand toe to toe and still be able to need you."

"Human beings are imperfect and therefore are incapable of identifying perfection in another."

"Perhaps the perfect woman is the one who is completely at peace with her imperfections."

"[someone who]...wears a 25-year-old sweat-stained gardening hat or tiara with equal ease…and knows which one to wear to meet the Queen."

"Humans must strive to locate others who balance our differences and thus create a good partnership."

"That would depend on each man. Some men like women who are dolled up compared to others who can't stand that type of woman. Some like women on the quieter side while others gravitate towards the life of the party. Then there are those who would never be with a woman unless she's a good cook and great homemaker, while others are capable of and enjoy doing that themselves. Is there really such a thing as the perfect woman? Just about as much as there's the perfect man."

"Makes enough money to give her husband some anxiety about his manhood."

"Best keep them to myself. ;0" [a man wrote this one]

"The perfect woman according to a Danish saying is someone who: LOOKS like a young Girl, ACTS like a Lady, THINKS like a Man, and WORKS like a Horse.!!!!!! ME!!!!!!"

Jasmine sent this last suggestion. She often came over to watch me write this piece and told me I did not need to search any further. A friend posted on Facebook that if I did not end up concluding Jasmine was the perfect woman, I would be in a heap of trouble. Point taken. Let me see if I can weave a correct ending to this quest in the remaining pages.

Someone else sent me a photo of "The Quiet Woman Restaurant & Bar" in the United Kingdom. Today, many other pubs and hotels are sporting the "Quiet Woman" handle, including in California. Although I recognize "quietness" is an attribute some men, and at least one songwriter, might have for their version of the perfect woman, I think I will step around that particular landmine.

Scientists have asked what constitutes perfection and have come up with what they think is the answer. Berkeley University professor Lior Pachter, a computational biologist working in genomics, investigated DNA. His study reveals a version of the genetically "perfect human." The criteria are complicated and have mostly to do with a propensity towards disease and numerous medical conditions. According to Pachter, *she* comes from Puerto Rico, where the population is often a mixture of European, West African, and Native American.

Rather than immediately visualizing Jennifer López, Pachter suggests thinking about the legendary Yuiza, a female chief of one of the indigenous tribes. When the Spanish *conquistadores* killed off most of the men, Yuiza took over as chief and took steps to protect the survivors. The legends do not tell of this perfect woman leading warriors into battle, killing the Spanish, but instead becoming a *conquistadores*' lover. Her reward? The other chiefs killed her.

So much for the ability *to kill* being a scientifically-proven attribute of perfection. Worse yet, a contemporary painting of Yuiza shows an attractive young woman with eyes averted away from a Puerto Rican male artist. A recent female artist shows Yuiza looking right at the viewer. The female artist's painting is based upon a vision after Yuiza appeared before the artist in the middle of the night.

So, science and art have defined "The Perfect Woman," and we can visualize either J. Lo or someone's idea of Yuiza. But are there enough Puerto Rican women in the world to go around, or should we encourage their population growth? Does this study finally end the historical nurture or nature debate? Does this mean Engels got not only Marxism wrong but also French women? I wonder whether Puerto Rican women post their DNA profiles on some secret Hispanophile social media site.

Biometric data collection should soon amass criteria able to match critical distances and features for individuals still hung up on physical attributes. Or perhaps governments have done that already with all of the computing power at their disposal. I mean, if they can track "persons of interest," why should we not assume that some bored technician has not tried to identify the perfect woman for his own personal interests? If you want someone who resembles J. Lo, or Catherine Deneuve, it should be just a matter of time before some organization will be able to find the perfect look-alike for your concept of an ideal woman. Note: see reference to identical twins above.

Several serious academic books deal with the ideal woman. In general, such authors agree the concept of a perfect woman depends upon the specific culture and the time. For example, the Indian goddess Sita would be ideal for the Hindu culture. The Virgin Mary might be the same for some Christians. References exist to various religious teachings, and many articles do not separate woman from wife or mother. I thought I could duck the subject of motherhood, but I find I cannot.

Before science told us it could explain everything, humans often turned to some form of spiritual or religious practice for the meaning of life. Sure enough, advice on women is still contained in those sources. Christianity is still the world's largest religion. Divided by numerous practices, a central point of general agreement is on *The Bible*. The main portion of *The Bible* dealing with the ideal or perfect woman is Proverbs 31. The passage relates what his mother told King Lemuel. The question is whether the passage refers to a woman of noble character or a wife. Such a person is worth far more than rubies, but the passage implies a woman cannot be noble unless she is a wife. There are many attributes for such a woman: running the household like a business, charity, bringing respect to the family, strength, dignity, wisdom, and being God-fearing. The passage cautions beauty is fleeting. This passage from the *Old Testament* is accepted in Judaism and is recited in the home. There are numerous Bible study groups, books, pamphlets, etc., that keep this passage alive.

The world's second-largest religion, Islam, also contains advice on what constitutes the perfect woman. Only four women in history could measure up to the high standards required of perfection under Islam. Such women were charitable, feeling of others, cheerful, magnanimous, and idealistic. Similar to the Christian view? Muslim women, of course, must be devoted to their religion. Under Muslim dress codes, women are freed from following materialistic fashions and shallow Western definitions of perfection. Male believers are cautioned that, if they marry her for anything other than a woman's religious piety, the marriage is bound to fail. Believers are told beauty and charm are hard to resist, but beauty does not last forever. Religious teachings remind men that beauty does not guarantee a woman's obedience and religiousness.

Sita, the wife, is the ideal woman for Hindus. She is recognized for her obedience and having followed her husband through many ordeals and resisted temptation from another man. Modern articles offering advice to young women remind them of the need to obey and sacrifice above all else. Not a lot of contemporary discussion about throwing yourself on a funeral pyre when the Lord and Master passes. Five *Panchakanya* characters in Hindu epics are traditionally considered ideal women. Common aspects of their stories are dealing with loss, being rewarded for good behavior, punishing adultery, and challenging men. In the fictional film *The Best Exotic Marigold Hotel*, we are reminded in a traditional Indian family that almost all marriages are arranged. I guess the selection of a perfect woman for a young man is beyond his innate capabilities. I wonder whether Hindu parents know about this sheep-killing thing.

Buddha did not envisage a subordinate role for women. A few academic articles claim ancient Asian societies could not accept the freedoms resulting from Buddha's view. Advice on the perfect woman on one Internet site suggests adherence to the faith, morality, meditation, simplicity, modesty, kindness to all living things, respect, and enthusiasm. I need to find out whether the perfect woman on the farm in Sweden is a Buddhist.

What have I learned in looking into the subject of "The Perfect Woman"? Well, for me, the answer is Jasmine. But is Jasmine "The Perfect Woman" for any other individual? Would Jasmine have been "The Perfect Woman" for me in a past life? Apparently, she was. Jasmine checked out my past life profile before we started dating exclusively.

I remind the reader my new Norwegian friend Bjørn "liked" my Facebook posting where I mentioned the sheep-killing Swedish farmer was the perfect woman and would serve as the genesis of this essay. Who am I to tell Bjørn or Brit their criteria for "The Perfect Woman" are not the ones I use? One central point in Brit's favor is she considered Jasmine perfect enough for me. She introduced us.

It would appear a woman capable of compassionate mammalian ruminant slaughter is an acceptable (if somewhat esoteric) criterion, whereas a woman executing human homicide is not. Who knows, maybe "The Perfect Woman" for all of us in another reality *is* defined foremost by being a woman who kills her own sheep. Consider a post-apocalyptic world, for example.

My conclusion is that perfection is an assessment by a single individual within a specific culture and time. Although perfection need not be judged by anyone other than oneself, perfection determined by others often requires context and implies measurement. An abstract concept of perfection lacking context and quantification may be suitable for self-esteem and play well in San Miguel de Allende, but I submit it will not sway the admissions dean at Harvard.

Previously published in the online Literary Arts Website *The Basil O' Flaherty*, July 10, 2016, as an essay, http://thebasiloflaherty.weebly.com/archives3.html; in *Passages: A Corrales Writing Group Anthology*, Chris Allen and Sandi Hoover, eds., North Charleston, SC: CreateSpace, January 19, 2017, pp. 151-169, and in *Tickled*, March 31, 2017, https://tickled-inc.com/2017/03/31/the-perfect-woman-opinion-essay-by-jim-tritten/. The essay was awarded Second Place in the New Mexico Press Women, New Mexico Communication 2017 Contest, Feature Story—On-Line Publication.

POLISHED WITH LOVE

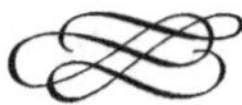

SANDI HOOVER

Cora Elizabeth Hood—Ettie, to her family, but Cora or Miss Hood to everyone else, was perhaps inordinately proud of being independent. She had completed high school, the first girl in the family to do so, and gone on to secretarial school to guarantee she could make a living. The Depression, in 1937, while not truly recovered from, was waning, businesses were hiring, and she found a job as a secretary in an architect's office.

There were several singles living in her Dallas boarding house. Most were, like Cora, escapees from rural or semi-rural backgrounds. They were products of strait-laced families now reveling in their freedom. They still maintained standards that would fall dramatically during the war. The girls worked for different companies; there were lots of junior members of firms as a mix and match for casual outings and dating.

They had groups who met for musical evenings in the clubs opened after Prohibition was repealed. Crowds of friends met on weekends to play tennis, an increasingly popular sport, or golf, the other excuse for mixed couples to be active together. There were dances and picnics, trips to the country with lots of car caravans, and crowds of young twenty-somethings enjoying freedoms they had never known before, Cora among them.

Imagine them, dressed in fashionable clothes, languidly reclining on plaid blankets, perhaps sipping a chilled sloe gin poured from a hip flask, sharing hopes for their futures.

"I shan't be a secretary all my career. I desire more than that," Cora said, feeling racy with a cigarette in hand.

"What do you think you'll do?" Mary, a close friend, asked, taking her seriously.

"Perhaps assistant to the partner. I'm a quick study. I'm thinking I'll read and study art and architecture books and be one of those who helps the designers." Cora stopped to drag on her cigarette.

Taller than most and opinionated, she seemed a tough nut to most men, but slowly she found a steady beau. Baker Whittington, sturdily built and taller even than Cora, challenged her at tennis, even though she won many of their matches. Keeping their competition even, he was a better golfer than she, but again, they were closely enough matched to keep the outcome in doubt.

"He calls me Helen when I win, referring to Miss Helen Wills Moody, but I'm certainly not her equal," she said to Mary as she brushed her midi-length skirt to rid it of dust as they left the tennis court after a practice session.

Mary nodded. "That's a lovely compliment since Miss Moody is a consummate professional and in the news all the time."

"It is, isn't it? In retaliation, I call him Paul when we play golf, and he's pleased to be compared to Mr. Runyan. He says he wishes he could make money at golf, but there are few pros surviving on their winnings, so he's keeping his job."

They giggled and headed for the YWCA to change clothes. Cora delighted in having Mary, more like a sister than a friend, to confide her ambitions, worries, and emotions regarding boyfriends. They were so different in size and style they felt no rivalry in the age-old dance to find a husband. Actually, they told one another they had no interest in marriage. A love, a lover, now that was something else again.

Cora was a head taller than Mary. Mary's small blonde roundness contrasted appealingly with Cora's elegant length of leg. Cora, though, was stunning in the long slender dresses which had replaced flappers' short skirts, and she considered slacks *a la* Katherine Hepburn the next thing.

As Baker and Cora chose to be a pair more often, it was assumed by their companions they had an understanding.

"We're talking seriously, and marriage is on the horizon," she divulged to Mary over a martini—one of the popular new drinks. No sweet, lady-drinks, as they called them. Those were old-fashioned.

Her secretarial job gave her money to spend after paying for her room and board, and she began filling her cedar hope chest with all the appropriate items for a girl who was engaged. Telling friends in detail how she and Baker had looked at jewelry stores and made decisions, she began adding a piece of her sterling each week on payday.

Baker was transferred to another city about this time, and Cora regaled her friends with tales of the letters she received and the plaintive yearning tone in his writings since being away from her. Her response to his absence was to increase her activities with girlfriends, letting the men know she was engaged to Baker and being faithful to him.

She took a train trip, and when she returned, she told her friends Baker had requested a rendezvous, and they met in Chicago, a city big enough and far enough away from home in Dallas so they would be anonymous. Her friends were shocked, titillated, and scandalously excited for her. Her reputation as belonging to Baker was solidified as she spent more time alone, ostensibly pining for or writing to him.

"He says how much he misses me, so I can't not write back, can I? I don't want him waiting and hurting with loneliness, or worse yet, finding some floozy who'll comfort him."

Political tensions mounted as war broke out and expanded in Europe. Although President Roosevelt was attempting to keep the United States out of the conflict, it looked inevitable that U.S. involvement was on its way. The parties became less frequent and discussions sober as the potential heightened for many of the men to go to war.

When she was out with her girlfriends, Cora talked lengthily about Baker's desire to participate in the war he saw coming and his resolution to be among the first to sign up—in spite of her protests.

Mary frequently bore the brunt of Cora's anguish. "He's being so foolish. Why doesn't he wait to see if he will have to go? Men! They love the idea of being heroes. They forget the painful parts. My father was in the last war, and my mother says he's not been the same ever since."

The surprise attack on Pearl Harbor in 1941 shocked Cora and all her friends. Life was now very serious with the United States declaring war on Japan. Dallas had few Japanese, and the idea Japan would attack the U.S. was hard to comprehend. They barely absorbed the reality of war with Japan when, eleven days later, Germany declared war on the United States, and America answered in kind.

Cora had red-rimmed eyes and constantly sniffled from tearing up, and she could be heard sobbing in the ladies' room. She carried a wadded handkerchief in one hand with which to dab her eyes.

"I haven't heard from him in two weeks. I despair of getting his letter. I know he will have joined the Navy. That was his first choice. I dread what I will read."

"Cora, crying won't stop Baker from signing up. You've got to get a hold of yourself," Mary advised.

Less than three weeks after the United States responded to the European war declaration, she told her friends that Baker had signed on to the Navy and was going for training almost immediately.

"I must go to Colorado to see him. We will be separated by a greater distance soon. He says he has been told to report for duty. She sniffled and continued, "I haven't had the heart to look at a map to know where that is." Her voice rose as it ended in a near cry, and she turned and dashed for the restroom again.

Her distraction reflected itself in her work that week, so when her boss suggested she take time, take a bus to Colorado where Baker was living and see him off to report for duty, she leaped at the chance.

"Thank you for understanding," she told him. "I promise I'll be back to my usual self when I return." She caught a Greyhound bus that night after work and was gone for nearly a week. She was thinner and wan, although she seemed happier when she returned wearing a ring.

"He's gone to war, but I will wait for him to come back to me," she said as she wiped her eyes once more.

The war dragged on, and weeks became months, with Cora describing in detail Baker's letters to anyone who would listen.

"The censors make it hard to be sure where he is, but since he talks about being cold, I think his ship is in the Atlantic," she said.

The war years continued, and Cora spoke of Baker less and less. She realized her friends were tired of hearing her sagas of his letters, and several of their good friends from the group had been killed in action. In late 1944 she told them he had been transferred to the Pacific theater to join a ship in the fleet in the Philippines, as closely as she could guess, based on the things said in newspapers.

On a cold Monday in January, Cora hysterically called the company switchboard, "I can't come in today. My fiancé has been reported missing since his ship was sunk." Telling the operator who to notify, she burst into tears and hung up. She called in the next day as well but appeared at the architectural firm on Wednesday with bleary red eyes and an ashy complexion. Cora's friends hugged her, and the men avoided her, hoping not to provoke an outburst.

"I'm not going to talk about Baker. I'm sure he's alive somewhere but can't let me know. He'll be back, I know it," she said.

Resolutely, she bent to her job, excelling in all the tasks she was given. Time passed with no word from Baker, no words from Cora regarding him; Japan surrendered, and the world went to work trying to forget the past years. Business increased, and she was promoted several times as she became more valuable to the firm.

Mary, and others of Cora's group, married. Her younger brothers also married and had children, but Cora never encouraged men she met, remaining steadfast to her memory of Baker.

She contracted lung cancer—dying in 1977, having never married.

Her papers, photos, and things the family deemed valuable were collected in boxes and stored in her brother George's attic. There they rested until the house owned by her brother was sold as he and his wife moved into a nursing home. Those several boxes made the move, with her brother's flotsam, to the next generation's house, and then one more move to a grandson's home. Their large garage had space to stack "Great-Aunt Cora's things," as the boxes were now labeled, waiting next to "George/Granddad's Stuff" for some occasion to demand their examination and winnowing.

That time came when Cora's great-great-niece, Elizabeth May Hood, the only daughter, was moving from a college dorm room to her first apartment. Her family started searching for things necessary to create her nest and remembered those boxes. They were exhumed from the dusty back corner of the garage where they had kept company with George's residual boxes.

"While we are at this, it's time to deal with all these leftovers. There's no point in having them fill up a corner of the garage when they can be used—or just thrown away," said Martin, Elizabeth's dad, as he looked at the eight cartons that represented Cora's life. "It's hard to realize my dad's life and hers can be contained in less space than we use for the cars."

"We'll start at the edge and work our way through these cartons. Time for memories and time to appreciate who they were."

The first of Cora's boxes to be opened contained books and a few important papers, along with awards from her workdays or the volunteer organizations she spent time on. The books were being sorted to be given to the library or Goodwill when Elizabeth found two cloth-covered journals.

She opened one and read the title, *Personal Diary of Cora Elizabeth Hood, begun on the date Nov 5, 1936*, all in fancy script. The second was simpler, *Cora Elizabeth's Diary, The War—*. There was no ending date.

"I'm going to take time out to read some of great-aunt Cora's writing. You and mom can feel free to leave the rest of her boxes for me to do when I am through with this reading break," Elizabeth said, carrying the faded fabric books with her and heading into the house.

With a glass of iced tea in hand, she sat in the cozy chair in her old room, now only used on brief trips home but still full of familiar things and memories of almost recent high school. After a few sentences, she was immersed in Cora's old-fashioned writing and wordy stories of the brand new life she was living in a boarding house, having finished secretarial school. As she skimmed through the bits and pieces, she smiled as she shared Cora's success and thrill in getting a good job with an architectural firm still recognizable as a large influence in central Texas.

Soon she was immersed in Cora's life—meeting people, making friends, the excitement of being independent. There were lots of details of outings and parties, fragile clippings tucked here and there, more word pictures of friends, their likes and habits, appearances, and quirky bits that caught Cora's imagination. And toward the end of the first book, Elizabeth's heart raced as she thrilled at Cora's infatuation with Baker Whittington. Elizabeth blushed, feeling like a voyeur as she read details of their growing relationship. In late 1940, the writing changed. Elizabeth strained to read as Cora's writing became careless and not so legible.

First, Baker was transferred to Colorado, and their relationship had to endure separation. Cora wrote frequently but received few letters in return. As months passed, she complained to her diary even those few letters were diminishing further. She anguished over the idea he might have found someone else and be through with her.

Cora was despairing. She wrote letters to Baker that were not answered. Loving letters elicited no response. When war was declared in Europe, she was sure he would enlist at the first possible moment. She left streaks on pages from tears reflecting the strain she felt as she wrote about Baker's determination to volunteer for the war before he had to. The bleak line—*he's gone*—said it all.

Elizabeth wondered how much Cora really could have known of those ideas of Baker's. *Was there more communication, or did her imagination all conjure this? It's hard to know.* Elizabeth flipped some empty pages to the next writing.

Using vacation time after the New Year's holiday, Cora wrote an entry while on a bus to Colorado to his last address. *The scenery should be glorious, garbed as it is gleaming white, but it is simply stark to me—*

the stuff of nothingness. In Denver, she spoke to his landlady, who told her he had indeed joined the Navy and gone off to one of the training centers near the Great Lakes. Weeks had passed since he'd had friends come to a final party (the landlady said he'd been quite the party guy until she asked him to keep it quieter) at his rooms, and they took away the few things he'd acquired to add to a furnished set of rooms. That was all she knew.

Cora sat in a cheap hotel room and wrote about loneliness and abandonment. *My heart has been ripped out. How I long to hear Baker's voice. I miss our intimate conversations when we picnicked and spent lazy afternoons discovering things we valued in each other. We slept in one another's arms. How could he shut off our friendship, our love (I haven't made that up—have I?) without a word, without maintaining our honesty until the end? I can't stand it.* Her plaintive writing continued in the same vein for several pages as she poured out her anguish, wondering where he was and how he felt. *What will I tell my friends?*

Further on, she complained to her diary how few hours of sleep she had gotten, and the last page about her trip described her visit to a jewelry shop. She wrote of admiring the lovely things being created with new modern designs, unlike her mother's pendants and rings. Then she added a story about the storm delaying the bus from leaving for a day and the additional stress of waiting and waiting in the station to get back home.

Fatigue. I never knew a body could be so tired. These leaden legs cannot move again. She wrote and slept on the bus, waking only when the bus stopped to let passengers off or on. Elizabeth moved to the second book.

It was a surprise. The first pages started with comments about Baker's letters, infrequent because he was at sea and couldn't get or send mail with regularity. She described her engagement ring. Cora regaled her diary with flowery language of love from his letters. *His heart is heavy with remorse that we had no time before he left to see one another, to kiss, to hug, and more. He is fearful of German U-boats and wishes he were on solid ground.*

Many pages were filled with Baker, with stories of his enduring the war from a ship, and his need for her, her laughter, and their love. Less frequent but revealing were her comments about the effects of the war on the civilian population. She mentioned rationing and stockings being unavailable. She laughed at Mary's vanity since she drew a pencil line on her calf to mimic the seam in stockings. *Not for me, this phony attempt to dress up. I go bare-legged with pride in helping the war effort. Is worrying about Baker a help to the effort? I constantly pray for his safety.*

Elizabeth scanned pages and flipped forward, hunting for the end of the story. What happened to Cora? Elizabeth hadn't known her, being born in 1996, but she was interested now in someone who was independent at a time when most women stayed home. She read where Cora took a war leave from the architect since business was limited, and she worked in a factory packing parachutes.

Silver is now exorbitantly expensive. I have stopped adding to my trousseau and will wait until Baker is home to finish the silverware settings. We can complete it hand in hand. Cora added that since the European theater was nearing collapse, Baker and his ship were now near the Philippines, where so much of the action was happening.

There were a few more pages lamenting his absence, and then the journal ended with a page mostly scribbles and a few, hard to translate, words. Elizabeth sat with a bright light on the book and a magnifying glass, trying to decipher the faded writing.

After straining over it, she thought some of it said Baker was dead. The rest was unintelligible and perhaps not even words. *Hysterical scratchings?* she wondered.

Now totally intrigued, Elizabeth found her laptop and started an online hunt for Cora's beau. She examined the National Archives for Texas and Colorado, not only the wounded, dead and missing, but also the draft records and all the other leads she could find. Then she broadened her search. There was no notice anywhere of a Baker Whittington. "I'm glad his name wasn't Smith. This experiment would be impossible," Elizabeth said to herself as she scrolled through another short listing of *W*s in the missing category. A final thought struck her. She entered Colorado death notices and then followed the trail from the Denver Public Library's death index.

"Oh, no." Elizabeth gasped as she found Baker Whittington listed on Dec 28, 1941. Stunned and in tears for a man she didn't know, she found the Denver Post archives and searched December of 1941, feeling like a detective tracking down a fugitive. A fugitive who turned out possibly not to have abandoned Cora but by dying had the decision removed from his hands. She scrolled through several obituaries before she found his name.

Baker Whittington, a resident of Denver, was killed instantly yesterday when he stepped into the path of a city bus. No known next of kin. His orders to report to Great Lakes, Illinois, were in his coat pocket, along with an unfinished letter to a female friend. Our Naval Service has lost a fine young man.

Elizabeth bowed her head over her keyboard and mused out loud. "This was not the ending I was prepared for. Aunt Cora may have made up the intensity of his feelings, but here is a reason she never heard from him again. I'd like to think the letter he was carrying was to her."

Closing her laptop, her breathing shaky, she carried the journals back to the garage where her mom and dad had concentrated their cleaning efforts on George's effects. More boxes from the back corner of the garage were filling the spaces usually occupied by cars.

"Well, did you enjoy the memoir you took to your room? What did you learn about the old girl? I was too young to remember her, but dad said she was pretty feisty and an outspoken, independent woman back in the day," Martin said with a smile. He and Phyllis, her mom, sat down on a couple of folding chairs, using Elizabeth as an excuse to rest.

Elizabeth sat too, with the journals on her lap, “I wouldn’t say enjoy, but her journals are interesting. They created an image of her youth. I think she went through life with a broken heart, so the writing makes me sad. She had a pretense for friends that her beau was alive on a ship and would come back to her until she ‘killed him off’ before the war ended because she hadn’t heard from him. What really happened—her boyfriend was killed in a street accident as the U.S. joined the war after the attack on Pearl Harbor. She never knew.”

“Oh honey, that’s tragic. I’ve seen photos of Cora, and I always thought she had sad eyes,” Phyllis said.

“The story and her writing make her special to me. Feeling abandoned could haunt your every day and create shadows on happiness. Today, it would be hard for someone to die without friends knowing. We have instant communication and connectedness, but things before the war took longer to go to and fro and could get lost along the way.” Elizabeth stood and put the journals on the chair she’d left.

She turned to the remaining boxes. “We’ve been through papers and books. Let’s see what else is here to tell us about Cora.” She picked up the dust cloth where she had thrown it over the back of the chair. “These haven’t been touched in a while, and under the dust, the tape is coming loose. Dusting is definitely a priority.”

“Achoo!” She sneezed as she stirred the dust on the tops of the remaining cartons with the damp rag.

“OK, it’s time to unpack her bits and pieces. Sadly, they weren’t used as planned,” Elizabeth commented as she unwrapped china plates and bowls and arranged them on the folding table now emptied of books. “Her china is a bit old-fashioned but still quite serviceable. She used it for years. The wear and tear are obvious.”

At the bottom of the heaviest carton was one last object. She lifted out a cloth-wrapped silver chest. Opening the box, Elizabeth gasped in surprise. “This silverware is simply elegant and timeless. Whether you bought these for yourself, or you and Baker truly chose this pattern—Cora, I will treasure these in your memory and polish them with love.”

Previously published in *Love, Sweet to Spicy: A Corrales Writing Group Anthology*, Patricia Walkow and Christina G. Allen, eds., North Charleston, SC: CreateSpace, Jan 21, 2018, pp. 95-106.

ACKNOWLEDGMENTS

Our thanks to the past and present members of the Corrales Writing Group—Chris Allen, John Atkins, Maureen Cooke, Tom Neiman, and Pat Walkow—for their constant support and insightful critiques of our work.

Heading the list of supporters, we are grateful to our spouses—Richard Hoover and Jasmine Tritten—who bear the brunt of reading drafts and gently proffer ideas, corrections, and changes.

ABOUT THE AUTHORS

Sandi Hoover

Sandi has always been fascinated by animals, plants, and birds. Her childhood behind-the-scenes experiences during Summer Zoo School at the San Diego Zoo reinforced her enthusiasm. She spent her working career as executive director of the Houston Audubon Society and then the Bayou Preservation Association, both active conservation non-profit organizations. While those positions led to interesting activities, her writing was specific and pragmatic. There was no humor or fiction involved in position papers and environmental statements. Before joining the Corrales Writing Group, her avocational writing was confined to personal travel journals and descriptive letters to family and friends, plus the occasional article for local newsletters. Since procrastination is easy—seemingly, only deadlines prompt action—joining the Corrales Writing Group has demanded the discipline of writing on a regular basis. Learning the craft of writing in a more formal way through presentation, followed by critique from this trusted group of friends, has provided a safe place to learn new skills and grow as an author.

A birder and naturalist, she enjoys watching and analyzing wildlife's behavior, trying to understand how they fulfill their basic needs. Her writings frequently reflect her interest in the natural world. Indulging her curiosity about nature has inspired trips to experience wilderness firsthand. From King Eiders in Barrow, Alaska, to King Penguins on South Georgia Island, seeing animals in their natural habitat has been a life-long pursuit. She still gazes out her office window or pets her cat (always kept safely indoors) instead of writing.

~

Jim Tritten

Jim retired after a forty-four-year career with the Department of Defense, including duty as a carrier-based naval aviator. He holds advanced degrees from the University of Southern California and formerly served as a faculty member and National Security Affairs department chair at the Naval Postgraduate School. Dr. Tritten's publications have won him fifty writing awards, including the Alfred Thayer Mahan Award from the Navy League of the U.S. He has published eight books and over three hundred chapters, short stories, essays, articles, and government technical reports. Jim was a frequent speaker at many military, arms control, and international conferences and has seen his work translated into Russian, French, Spanish, and Portuguese.

www.ingramcontent.com/pod-product-compliance
Lightning Source LLC
Chambersburg PA
CBHW021203020426
42331CB00003B/189

* 9 7 8 1 6 3 7 7 7 1 0 8 2 *